Working with the Core Relationship Problem in Psychotherapy

Althea J. Horner

Foreword by

Samuel Slipp

Working with the Core Relationship Problem in Psychotherapy

A Handbook for Clinicians

Jossey-Bass Publishers • San Francisco

Substantial discounts on bulk quantities of Jossey-Bass books are available to corporations, professional associations, and other organizations. For details and discount information, contact the special sales department at Jossey-Bass Inc., Publishers (415) 433–1740; Fax (800) 605–2665.

For sales outside the United States, please contact your local Simon & Schuster International Office.

Jossey-Bass Web address: www.josseybass.com

 Manufactured in the United States of America on Lyons Falls Turin Book. This paper is acid-free and 100 percent totally chlorine-free.

Library of Congress Cataloging-in-Publication Data

Horner, Althea J.
    Working with the core relationship problem in psychotherapy : a handbook for clinicians / Althea J. Horner.
        p.   cm. — (The Jossey-Bass psychology series)
    ISBN 0-7879-4301-0 (hc : alk. paper)
    1. Object relations (Psychoanalysis)   2. Psychodynamic psychotherapy.   I. Series.
    [DNLM: 1. Object Attachment.   2. Interpersonal Relations.
3. Psychoanalytic Theory.   4. Psychoanalytic Therapy.
WM 460.5.02 H816W 1998]
616.89'17—dc21
DNLM/DLC
for Library of Congress   97-52693

HB Printing   10 9 8 7 6 5 4 3 2 1   FIRST EDITION

Contents

Foreword

This book provides a unique perspective on how we can help our patients deal with their emotional problems. Althea Horner combines the best attributes of a writer. She is both clear and profound. She offers both the latest theoretical knowledge and help with the practical issues confronting therapists in their work with their patients. Thus this book deals with both a general overall framework and specific issues that enable us to provide the best psychotherapeutic care for our patients.

We know that the original Freudian theory denied the attachment to the mother in early childhood development and focused on drives, as if the infant were isolated in a cocoon. The theory was male oriented, even for female children. Freud considered the superego to be structured *only* by internalization of the father after resolution of the oedipal complex. We now know from direct infant observation and other research that attachment to the mother occurs very early after birth and that the mother forms the core of the infant's psyche. Modern theory of child development is panphasic, from pre-oedipal to young adult relationships, and it describes how the interpersonal process leads to structure in the personality.

In this book, Horner makes a unique contribution by emphasizing the patient's *core relationship problem*. The core relationship problem is formed during childhood and creates an internalized mental image of the self in relation to others. This relationship image, with its associated feelings, thoughts, and desires, then determines adult perceptions, expectations, and interpersonal relations. Understanding the core relationship problem becomes essential in treatment.

In addition to addressing individual development, Horner reviews the influence of family systems pathology. Unresolved issues and fantasies within the parents may be placed into one or more children through projective identification. This identification in turn influences how the child experiences himself or herself and relates to others. Horner also reviews the importance of the broad belief and value systems found in the culture and their effect on individual psychopathology.

This book then focuses its lens down to working with some difficult types of psychopathology and some problematic issues that often arise during the course of psychotherapy. For example, what does the therapist do when a patient requests hugging, gives gifts, or resents paying for therapy because he or she wants to feel special? It also deals with transference and countertransference issues as well as some patients' taboos on winning in encounters with a parent or a therapist, issues that prevent progress in treatment.

One excellent chapter discusses the importance of dealing with termination issues. Another chapter clearly elucidates the special problems affecting the relationship when the therapist works with patients under managed care. Finally, a chapter devoted to supervisors of therapists explores many issues that may arise during supervision—for example, the *parallel process*, in which certain reactions evoked in the therapist by the patient are repeated in the relationship between the therapist and the supervisor.

Any therapist, whether beginning or experienced, will find a rich fund of knowledge to help him or her understand and deal with patients in this remarkably well-written book.

May 1998   Samuel Slipp
Clinical Professor of Psychiatry
New York University
School of Medicine

Preface

This book has come out of my work with several consultation groups over a number of years. I have observed that certain clinical issues come to the fore again and again, especially certain aspects of early psychological development and the later psychopathologies related to them. Certain questions about understanding the patient and doing the work have tended to come up repeatedly over time in connection with a large variety of cases presented.

I have found that I often have occasion to refer to the extensive research of Luborsky, Crits-Christoph, Mintz, and Auerbach (1988), who address the question of who will benefit from psychotherapy and who have found that a patient benefits most when a therapist correctly identifies his or her *core relationship problem*, regardless of the presenting problem. This core relationship problem is set up with the primary caretaker(s) in a patient's early, most formative years. Many therapists tend to become embroiled with the patient's marital or work problems: that is, they work with the derivatives of the developmental conflicts, neglecting how the individual came to this way of being in the world in the first place. They do not address the deeper underlying, unconscious wishes, fears, and conflicts that are acted out and manifested in the here-and-now situation. I liken this approach to looking in the mirror, seeing you have dirt on your nose, then taking a piece of tissue and trying to wipe the mirror clean.

Purpose and Approach

The purpose of this book is to assist therapists in identifying the patient's core relationship problem early in the treatment and to use this problem as the organizing principle for understanding the later derivatives and the many layers of adaptive, expressive, and defensive elaboration that have accrued over the years. The core problem will involve issues around attachment, dependency, individuation, and autonomy and the ways in which they may have become convoluted, double binding, or mystifying, leading to a variety of developmental pathologies and defenses. These pathologies and defenses may be imbued with issues of pride and shame or eroticized within complex compromise formations. Oedipal issues also can be condensed into the core dynamic.

This approach of working with the core relationship problem is an elaboration of my object relations orientation (Horner, [1979] 1984, 1991b). This orientation posits that *each stage along the developmental line running from birth through attachment, separation, and individuation and through later development in childhood and adolescence has its own developmental tasks and stage-specific and appropriate requirements of the caretaking environment. Each stage also has its own pitfalls, where significant failure of that environment will leave lasting effects on the individual's character structure and on the manner in which he or she connects with others and then continues to relate to them.* That is, structural pathology and relationship conflicts can arise at any of these stages.

In this book, I shift the emphasis from what is structural to what is dynamically relational. However, in order to provide the reader with an overview of the early developmental stages from the structural perspective as well as with what is required in the relationship with the primary caretaker in each stage, I begin the book with a revised version of a previously published chapter (Horner, 1987) that introduces the concept of the unconscious and the archaeology of human relationships.

When we use the term *psychic structure*, we refer to an enduring organization of psychological elements. *Enduring* is the salient word here. The term *self representation* is a structural concept. In healthy development the self-representation comes to encompass all aspects of the psycho-physiological self: somatic experience, affect, impulse, perception, and thought. There is an integration of all these aspects under the umbrella of what we call the *self*. A corresponding structure, the *object representation*, develops hand in hand with the self representation. The development of these mental structures takes place in the context of the primary caretaking relationship as well as in the context of built-in schedules of maturation. Interpersonal experience is thus structured and becomes established intrapsychically, and what is then intrapsychic is expressed interpersonally. Core relationship problems that arise early in life thus have a structural underpinning.

The term *object relations* is also a structural concept. Object relations refers to the inner mental structures of the self and object representations and their dynamic interplay, along with associated characteristic feelings, wishes, and fears. The object relationship situation, the inner psychological structure, becomes manifest in interpersonal relationships, the transference being one that is of particular interest to the therapist.

In this book the focus is on these interpersonal, or relationship, manifestations of the intrapsychic structure. *Relational* is a generic term applying to the interpersonal aspect of many theories. Sullivan (1956), who described his perspective as an *interpersonal theory* and elaborated it through his own unique concepts, wrote that "it is in that process by which the human animal is converted into a human being . . . that there comes about a great differentiation of the goals of behavior and therefore of the integrating tendencies that characterize interpersonal relations" (p. 10). The concept of psychic structure—as useful as I believe it to be—keeps us in an intellectual stance, but the relationship way of thinking brings us into the realm of flesh-and-blood experience. The structure is, in effect, a mental scaffolding upon which later development through childhood and adolescence builds and is organized. Furthermore, the core relationship problem can arise later as well as earlier along the developmental continuum.

Expanding the Limits of Theory

The reader will observe that I go outside the limits of object relations theory, consistent with my long-standing efforts to integrate new psychoanalytic ideas into the existing mass of psychoanalytic wisdom, to approach new ideas in an attitude of creative synthesis. I have taken this same approach to the limits of psychoanalytic theory in general as well. Starting with the same observations of human behavior, each theory organizes these data according to different principles. One form of organization may be no more "true" than another. We may think in terms of psychosexual stages, in terms of Mahlerian stages of separation and individuation, or in terms of Eriksonian stages of the individual in relation to society. We may think in terms of Freudian oedipal conflict, Kohutian reaction to failure of empathy, Winnicottian false self adaptation to impingement, or even Skinnerian shaping. My background of clinical psychology, with its own body of knowledge and concepts, enriches and is enriched by psychoanalytic ideas. The work of Piaget; family systems theory; the philosophy of Buber and the importance of the I-thou encounter; existential questions concerning being itself; language and thought; and the search for meanings embedded in ordinary words—none of these are psychoanalytic concepts, yet they enhance our psychoanalytic work if we allow them into our *creative synthesis*. The reader who seeks to place the concepts in this book into a single theoretical classification is likely to be disappointed. Though theory is our guide, it must not be our God, and it is the concretization of theory and its consequent doctrinaire rigidity that has led postmodern thinkers to question the value of theory itself. I choose not to throw the proverbial baby out with the bath water.

Finally, the examples in this book are fictional composites that draw from a wide number of cases and situations. Because no two people are alike (being as idiosyncratic as their fingerprints or their DNA), as much as specific cases elucidate they can also mislead when applied to other situations. I have tried in this book to draw from a variety cases, so as to communicate to the reader more *a way of thinking* than a directory of what to do. There are no formulas, and the therapist must turn to his or her own intelligence, intuition, and ability to synthesize creatively when making use of the ideas presented here or elsewhere. I find that beginning therapists tend to look for rules to follow—never do this and always do that—out of their own anxiety and wish for certainty. To be a psychotherapist is to commit oneself to a lifetime of learning, and it is my hope that this book will make its own small contribution to that process.

My thanks to Alan Rinzler for his help in organizing the manuscript.

May 1998   Althea J. Horner
                                                  Pasadena, California

The Unconscious and the Archaeology of Human Relationships

I come to my thoughts about mental development and the nature of the unconscious as a biological scientist. The marriage between biology and philosophy may appear strange and unnatural, but insofar as all aspects of being are integrated within a cohesive self in healthy development, a person's biology, psychology, and philosophy must inevitably and permanently be wedded.

Because that which we call the *unconscious* cannot be directly perceived, it must be considered a theoretical construct. Adler (1980), referring to the *electron* in nuclear physics and to the *black hole* in astronomy, notes that modern science legitimately and validly deals with objects that lie outside the range of ordinary experience because they cannot be directly perceived. He describes the unconscious in psychology as a similarly legitimate and valid object of study (p. 67). He also reminds us of Ockham's assertion that "we are justified in positing or asserting the real existence of unobserved or unobservable entities if—and *only* if—their real existence is indispensable for the explanation of observed phenomena" (p. 98).

Strachey (1957) wrote that the basis of Freud's repression theory of hysteria and the cathartic approach to treatment "cried out for a psychological explanation," noting that it was "only by the

---

The author gratefully acknowledges permission to reprint this chapter, with slight adaptations, which was originally published in Raphael Stern (ed.), *Theories of the Unconscious and Theories of the Self*, pp. 27–39. Copyright © 1987 The Analytic Press, Hillsdale, N.J.

most contorted efforts that they had been accounted for neurolog-
ically" (p. 164). The neurological explanation disappeared in
Freud's *Interpretation of Dreams* ([1900] 1953b), and what Freud had
written previously about the nervous system he now translated into
mental terms. Strachey says that here "the unconscious was established once and for all" (p. 164). Nevertheless, the neurological-
psychological controversy still flourishes today (as discussed in
Chapter Seven).

Freud ([1915] 1957c) saw the difficulties of "psycho-physical
parallelism" as insoluble, the physical characteristics of "latent
mental states" being totally inaccessible to us. "No physiological
concept or chemical process can give us any notion of their nature"
(p. 168). "On the other hand," he adds, with respect to these mental states, "we know for certain that they have abundant points of
contact with conscious mental processes." Setting his role as neu-
rologist aside, he says that "every endeavor to think of ideas as
stored up in nerve cells and of excitation as traveling along nerve
fibers, has miscarried completely" (p. 174).

Despite findings of recent brain research concerning the functioning of neurotransmitters and involving direct visualization of
the brain at work, we are really no further along than Freud in our
understanding of the physical correlates of what we call *mind*. But
as long as we speak as scientists, we must assume that like the black
hole, they are there. And as long as they remain unknowable, the
theoretical construct we refer to as the unconscious allows us to
bridge what is unknown with what is known.

The Stages of Object Relations

When they work from an *object relations* point of view, therapists
and patients seek to discover the content of the unconscious that
most directly affects the experience of the self, the experience of
the other, and the complex relationships between them.

A developmental approach to the understanding of these experiences of self and other (experiences that include ideas, percep-

tions, feelings, wishes, and impulses) has taken us back further and further in the life of the child, with most recent research highlighting the interactional basis of their evolution from the start of life. As genetically patterned as the hunting and mating behaviors of other species is the neonate's readiness to respond to, and also to initiate, that interaction. Also built into the healthy central nervous system is the readiness to respond to patterns and actively to construct and synthesize new patterns.

The patterning of the mental schema we call *self* and the patterning of the mental schema we call *object* take place in predictable, hierarchical stages. We use the term object rather than *mother* because this particular mental schema is in part *created* by the child in accord with its own limited mental capabilities and unique experience of the early caretaking environment. The child creates a kind of metaphor and images for the significant other from its interpersonal experiences. This metaphor then reciprocally shapes the child's perception and expectations of the interpersonal environment, along with the child's behavior toward it. Herein lies the relevance of unconscious mental schemata for conscious experience and behavior and for the psychological treatment of disturbances in that sphere.

It is the child's ability to synthesize patterns out of experience and to register, as memory, those that occur repeatedly and regularly that leads from a *process* of interaction to what we call *psychic structure*—that is, to the enduring memories that will build and evolve over time to form the mental schemata of self and object. These patterns are built up out of the child's entire universe of experience, including what originates from within its own body as well as what originates from the external world with which it interacts.

The failure to distinguish between process and structure has led to some popular misconceptions about attachments, or what is often referred to as *bonding*. Rather than being understood as a process that leads eventually to structure, attachment is being understood as an *event*. Parents-to-be, as well as delivery-room personnel, espouse what might be characterized as the *epoxy theory of attachment,* believing that this is an event that takes place immediately in the first minutes of life, analogous to the imprinting experienced by Lorenz's ducks ([1935] 1957).

But we are not ducks, and although attachment-seeking behavior begins in the early hours with the maintenance of eye contact by the baby, the actual structuring of the *enduring mental tie* with the primary caretaker takes several months to develop fully. During this time, the child builds or synthesizes the experience of himself or herself in such a way as to include the primary caretaker (usually the mother) and the salient qualities of their interaction.

That the expectant mother who wants her baby is bonded to it long before it is born is clearly evident in the grief of women who miscarry. Yet the faddish furor over the critical nature of bonding and the near hysteria surrounding it has meant that some women who are unable to deliver by natural childbirth or who for some reason are unable to have immediate *skin-to-skin* contact with their new baby are inflicted with undue anxiety or guilt about themselves as mothers or about the future of their child.

As the child negotiates a series of developmental processes, beginning with the process of attachment, each stage brings him or her to a higher level of structural organization. The schemata of self and object—*self representation* and *object representation* in psychoanalytic terms—*become increasingly complex and increasingly differentiated* from each other. At the same time, disparate aspects of the organization of the self become increasingly integrated within a single self-schema while a similar process takes place with disparate aspects of object representation. Gradually, a single, integrated self representation evolves, as does a single, integrated object representation. However, even though we may speak of a single, integrated self representation, that self is exceedingly complex and various aspects may be in conflict with each other. In Chapter Eight, I describe working with dissociated self-states and address the current controversy over the nature of integration. Each level of psychic organization determines to a large extent the nature of the child's experience of himself or herself and of the other, along with the interaction between the two. This psychic organization is not directly observable, and for the most part it remains beyond conscious awareness, although what derives from it is conscious. Edith Jacobson (1964) defines *identity* as the conscious experience of the self-representation.

From the object relations point of view, the unconscious is highly organized, being characterized by a discoverable structure with its own dynamics, comparable to the dynamics of conscious experience. Discovering the link between them in the course of psychoanalytic therapy is the first step toward the remediation of pathological development and its consequent pathology of structure. Sandler (1981) notes that "every wish comes to include a representation of the person's own self and a representation of the object who also has a role to play in the fulfillment of the wish. The wish contains representations of self and object in interaction" (p. 183). The fact that such wishes are rooted in unconscious structure is what makes them so tenacious, to be acted out over and over even when the relationship may appear to the observer to be highly unsatisfactory.

Elsewhere (Horner, [1979] 1984) I have described the stages and processes in the development of early object relations and have related the pathology of each developmental way station to specific pathology of the personality. Particularly relevant to this discussion is the work of Mahler (1968; Mahler, Pine, and Bergman, 1975) and of Bowlby (1969), Winnicott ([1960] 1965a), and Kohut (1971). The remainder of this chapter describes these developmental stages, which are defined in terms of the self and object representations and their relationship to one another. Each stage leaves its traces in the unconscious, and even in the fully evolved individual, these traces may be reactivated under stress and regression or in dream or fantasy. As I noted in the Preface, my focus in this book is on what is dynamically relational as an interpersonal manifestation in the here and now of this intrapsychic representational world.

Preattachment Stage

At birth the child is in a state of what Mahler (1968) refers to as *normal autism* (p. 7). This term has been criticized because the newborn is clearly not in a chronic withdrawn state, as in pathological autism. Indeed, the child actively seeks contact from the very start. Here again the distinction between process and structure is important. Despite the immediate activation of the process of attachment, there is as yet no enduring, structured internal representation of the object. The experiences and their patterning and resultant memory traces are yet to come.

Grotstein (1990) wrote about "nothingness, meaninglessness, chaos and the 'black hole,'" traumatic states reported by patients that related to early infancy when the caretaking other failed in her holding capacity and when there was, as yet, no structured internal object to sustain the self. Some might argue that the infant's innate preference for the pattern of a facial configuration over a geometric or other nonhuman-type pattern (Fantz, 1966) indicates an innate object structure. However, although the precursors of self- and object representations may be present at birth in the form of *preference*, *readiness*, and *potential*, the cognitive development necessary for the structuring of the mental schemata and for the development of structure, as we use the term, has not yet occurred.

The most clearly stage-related pathology is that of early infantile autism, in which the child remains at the infantile stage of life and makes no move toward attachment. Along with the absence of attachment-seeking behavior, there appears to be a basic cognitive defect in these children that interferes with the organizational processes themselves. Before these discoveries, the mothers of such children were branded *icebox mothers*, on the assumption that the failure of attachment in these children was the direct consequence of the failure of the mother to facilitate the process. In situations in which the environment is grossly pathological, disrupting the organizing capacities of the child, there may be a retreat into secondary autism. Autistic withdrawal in response to severe stress in an adult suggests that similar failures of the environment date back to the earliest months of life. Similar autistic withdrawal in reaction to environmental failures would constitute the core relationship problem for that individual.

Process of Attachment Stage

Over the earliest months of life, we see the innate attachment-seeking behavior of the infant interacting with maternal behavior and response in a manner that, optimally, brings about the subsequent stage of normal symbiosis (Mahler, 1968), when the child has synthesized the experience of himself or herself in such a way as to include the primary caretaker and the salient qualities of their characteristic interaction. It is here that the basis for an affectional relationship and for what Erikson (1950) calls *basic trust* is laid down. The mother's emotional availability and her capacity for empathic response are essential to this process.

At the most primitive level, failure of attachment may carry with it severe deficits in the early organization of the self. The failure to develop an attachment and to achieve a satisfactory symbiosis because of environmental factors such as institutionalization or an unstable foster home situation may lead to the development of characteristic disturbances, such as an inability to keep rules, a lack of capacity to experience guilt, and an indiscriminate friendliness with an inordinate craving for affection and no ability to make lasting relationships (Rutter, 1974). Also, the *affectionless psychopath* (Bowlby, 1946) is characterized by the failure to develop the affectional bond that goes with attachment.

In Chapter One, I refer to the work of Alan Schore (1996) that demonstrates the neurological basis for the failure to develop a cohesive self in the first year of life and the critical nature of mother-infant interaction during that period, particularly eye contact. If there is a disruption of attachment due to separation and loss, subsequent development then depends upon the availability of a satisfactory substitute attachment object. Such interruption may lead to a lifelong schizoid detachment. Rutter says that "many (but not all) young children show an immediate reaction of acute distress and crying (. . . the period of 'protest'), followed by misery and apathy (the phase of 'despair')." There may be "a stage when the child becomes apparently contented and seems to lose interest in his parents ('detachment')" (p. 29). Rutter concludes that this syndrome is probably due to the disruption or distortion of the bonding process itself. At a later time in treatment the effects of such separations and losses can be identified as the core relationship problem.

Bowlby (1960) notes that the persistent longing of a young child for the lost love object is often suffused with intense generalized hostility: "There is no experience to which a young child can be subjected that is more prone to elicit intense and violent hatred for the mother than that of separation" (p. 24). The detachment is not permanent if the separation is not too long, but, Bowlby states, there is reason to believe that after prolonged and repeated separations during the first three years of life, detachment can persist indefinitely.

The quality of the child's experience during the attachment process and during subsequent separations and losses in the first three years of life builds into his or her inner world the unconscious feelings and expectations about the interpersonal world that will color all later developmental stages as well as future interpersonal relationships.

Normal Symbiosis Stage

Midway between the process of attachment and the separation-individuation process (Mahler, 1968) stands the primitive mental structure, the undifferentiated self-object representations. Owing to the young child's immature cognitive abilities, the undifferentiated images of the self and object are not yet integrated into single images. Instead, they are organized on the basis of the predominant feelings that go with the interactions between the self and the other. The good self- and object images are linked by positive feeling and mood. The bad self- and object images are linked by negative feelings and mood. Not until the cognitive development that will come toward the end of the second year of life will the disparate images be integrated into single cohesive representations of the self and of the other. If the good-bad split persists into adult life, it leads to an inability to hold on to relationships. When the other fails to be all good because of a failure to meet the wishes or needs or demands of the self, he or she then becomes all bad and is discarded or becomes the object of intense hatred.

Insofar as the primary caretaker has been able to lend herself to the child's unfolding, the experience vis-à-vis the other is part of the child's positive and trusting experience of the self. Herein lies the archaic unconscious basis for the experience of oneness that at times comes with a loved other. But whatever the ecstasy of that experience, it may also carry a charge of anxiety at the felt loss of separateness of the self.

The bipolarity of experience—that which is directed toward the self and that which is directed toward the other—exists from the beginning of life. It starts with the infant's alternating attention to what is happening within its own body and to the interpersonal environment that it seeks to engage. All through life, these conflicting pulls will be felt in one way or another, the intensity of the conflict dependent upon the security of the sense of self and the security within the interpersonal situation. The conflict is often expressed as existing between "being myself" (identity) and "being in a loving relationship" (intimacy) (Horner, 1990). Sometimes these two states are believed to be mutually exclusive, especially when the mother reacts to the child's growing separation and individuation from her as if they were an assault and destructive to her well-being.

No sooner is the symbiotic structure established intrapsychically with the organization of the undifferentiated self-object representations, than the child moves toward a new process, that of separation and individuation (Mahler, Pine, and Bergman, 1975).

Hatching Stage: The Beginning Step of Separation

Mahler (1968) emphasizes the importance of the optimal symbiosis for subsequent differentiation of the self schema, or self representation, from the object representation. "The more the symbiotic partner has helped the infant to become ready to 'hatch' from the symbiotic orbit smoothly and gradually—that is, without undue strain on his own resources—the better equipped has the child become to separate out and to differentiate his self representations from the hitherto fused symbiotic self-plus-object representation" (p. 18). During this process the mother functions as a frame of reference, a point of orientation for the individuating child. If this security is lacking, there will be a "disturbance in the primitive 'self-feeling' which would derive or originate from a pleasurable and safe state of symbiosis, from which he did not have to hatch prematurely and abruptly" (p. 19). That is, while the self representation remains intertwined with the object representation, the loss of the object and the sense of connection with that person evoke a sense of disorganization and dissolution of the self of which the object and the sense of connection are still a part.

When a person's unconscious psychic structure is dominated by this picture, the person may experience severe separation panics. These separations can be due to a break in the emotional connection with the significant other as much as to an actual physical separation. It is the sense of inner connectedness that remains critical and that is so insecure. (Later I describe an individual who clings to his object no matter what the personal cost.) Agoraphobia may develop when the individual's house or apartment serves as a kind of prosthesis, standing unconsciously for the needed object. In therapy we will understand this lack of security as the core relationship problem.

Practicing Stage: The Second Step
of Separation and Individuation

During the period when the child is approximately ten to sixteen months of age, his or her focus shifts increasingly to those functions that develop as a consequence of the maturation of the central nervous system, such as locomotion, perception, and learning. These are referred to as the *autonomous functions of the ego*. The child is also increasingly confronted with the experience and awareness of separateness from the mother. Her ready availability when the child needs her and the pleasure the child derives from the mastery of new abilities make small separations tolerable for the child. With the culmination of the practicing period around the middle of the second year, the toddler appears to be in an elated mood. This accompanies the experience of standing upright and walking alone. This peak point of the child's belief in his or her own magic omnipotence, Mahler (1968) tells us, "is still to a considerable degree derived *from his sense of sharing in his mother's magic powers*" (p. 20).

At this point in development the inner representation of self and the other are still in great part undifferentiated, and this can be the anlage of the pathological structure referred to as the *grandiose self*. If things go wrong in the child's subsequent relationship with his or her caretakers, at a time when the child has come to realize how relatively helpless and dependent he or she really is, the grandiose self is a defensive fallback position. The adult that the child becomes can deny anxiety and dependency wishes as long as this inflated omnipotent self is in charge. The other is no longer of any emotional consequence. Of course the person must go to great lengths to protect this illusion, and if it is threatened, as by poor grades in school or the loss of a job, the reaction will be severe, with the development of symptoms such as depression or suicidal behavior. Sometimes others must be debased or demeaned to protect this state of being. An attack on the grandiose self, as by an ill-advised interpretation, may evoke a paranoid reaction inasmuch as this illusion functions to hold the self together and in that way protects survival.

Echoes of the practicing period and its magic omnipotence in the unconscious sometimes lead to persisting beliefs about the magical nature of one's abilities. Learning to walk and talk does indeed come as by magic, unlike the conscious effort one must make to learn the vocabulary of a foreign language at school. I have worked with some patients who were clearly of superior intelligence and to whom early learning was effortless throughout the grade school years; paradoxically, they were far less secure about their abilities than people of lesser innate ability. They did not connect their abilities with that sense of conscious effort that can give a person a feeling of some control over what he or she can and cannot do. What comes by magic can also disappear by magic—one cannot rely on it.

Rapprochement Stage and the Rapprochement Crisis

At around the age of eighteen months the toddler becomes increasingly aware of his or her separateness from the mother and the mother's separateness from him or her. The child's experiences with reality have counteracted his or her overestimation of omnipotence, self-esteem has been deflated, and the child is vulnerable to shame. Furthermore, through dependence on the object, who is now perceived as powerful, the child is confronted with the relative helplessness of the self. There is an upsurge of separation anxiety and depressed mood. If on the one hand the other uses power in a benign and helpful manner, that power is the basis for the child's sense of security. If on the other hand parental power is experienced as being against the self, as something that is not only given but also withheld, the child learns to both hate and envy the power and will develop techniques to control it. Behind such controlling behavior lie insecurity and anxiety. This is a core relationship conflict that may be acted out in therapy vis-à-vis the therapist. The patient needs the therapist to be strong and to have the power to help him or her, but the patient may hate and envy that power as well.

The major concern of the person who struggles with problems associated primarily with this stage of development is the loss of the support, love, and approval of the other that is feared to result from the assertion of the person's own wishes or feelings. Still vulnerable to feelings of helplessness and shame, the person tends to idealize the other and see that other as having the power to protect the self from these painful feelings. The other may be a parent or perhaps a spouse or friend. This persisting dependent way of seeing the self and the other, and the expectations and demands that go with it, puts a strain on interpersonal relationships. Although the other may be idealized, he or she is also envied and feared and is blamed when things do not go well.

The *rapprochement crisis* is the developmental switch point that marks the shift from a sense of omnipotence to a sense of helplessness—from a sense of perfection to a sense of shame. When prior development has not gone well, the conscious awareness of the reality of separateness and the loss of omnipotence may be very traumatic. If there are deficits in the structural organization of the self and object representations, either as the result of unfavorable circumstances and experiences or as the result of some failure in the child's synthesizing capabilities, these deficits become evident at this time. The child, and the adult he or she becomes, is unable to negotiate the developmental demands, and symptomatic behavior such as anxious clinging develops.

The response of the environment to the child's growth has to allow for the child's strivings toward autonomy that conflict with the intensely felt dependency needs. The term rapprochement suggests the alternating moving away from the mother and returning to her for emotional refueling. Healthy parents do not have a need for the child to stay dependent and helpless or to be completely self-reliant. They can shift their way of relating to the child, being empathically in tune with the child's conflicting impulses and needs. Echoes of the rapprochement crisis are heard in adolescence, and the setup in the unconscious left over from the earlier childhood phase of development will affect the manner in which the young person negotiates the later developmental tasks. Anxiety over self-assertion or at the prospect of moving out of the parental home may come from the activation of unconscious rapprochement factors. The sense of self and other is still being determined by the unconscious self and object representations that were in existence at that early time and are still making themselves felt. In the course of psychotherapy with this person as an adult, this rapprochement crisis will be recognized as the core relationship conflict.

Achievement of Identity and Object Constancy Stage

The child is now developing language, and so the concepts of "Mama" and "Baby" are established at the start of the rapprochement period. This conceptual capability has an organizing and integrating effect. Unintegrated islands of disparate self representations become unified cognitively and structurally under each specific label, or symbol. Disparate object representations are similarly unified. There is a single self who may be good or bad, happy or angry, and a single object who may also be experienced in a number of different ways. This cognitive and structural integration sets the stage for an integrated sense of self, or identity, and an integrated view of the other. Although the child may be angry at his or her mother for some felt deprivation or failure of empathy, she is still mother, loved and valued in her own right and not only for what she can do for the child's self. In the earlier stage of development, before the cognitive achievement that brought the recognition that there is really just one self and one emotional mother, the self and object representations were split on the basis of the quality of feeling and emotion that went into the interaction. Mother was all good, idealized, and adored, or she was all bad and hated. The self in interaction with her was also split. With integration the complex, differentiated self and the sense of having a single identity come into being and provide a foundation for an unfolding individuality.

This is the point at which the capacity for *ambivalence* comes into being. Although ambivalence may be a developmental achievement, it can be emotionally painful and may be defended against by a *defensive* splitting, despite the integration that has taken place.

In healthy development, where there is a realistic picture of the other, relationships are increasingly defined on the basis of here-and-

now interaction, although certain wishes, attitudes, and expectations, as well as the quality of emotion, are still colored by the for-
gotten past. Although archaic self and object representations persist
in the unconscious, their impact is mitigated by the ascendency of
reality-dominated perception and thought. The unconscious images
may appear in dreams or in fantasy or may be recreated in artistic
productions. The fairy godmother and the wicked witch of the fairy
tales of childhood strike a familiar chord in children and adults alike,
resonating with the now unconscious split images that dominate the
earliest months of life. At times we may yearn for the blissful oneness
of symbiosis or chafe under what feels like engulfment in a relationship. But by and large our reality perceptions keep us firmly rooted in
our own individuality and that of the other.

Identification and Emotional Autonomy Stage

With the final stages of differentiation of self from object, certain
identifications with the object remain as part of the self. These
become part of the internal constant object. The baby needed the
mother to comfort it and relieve its anxiety. Now the capacity to
comfort oneself and to relieve one's own anxiety with a variety of
psychological mechanisms is part of the self, derived from what once
came from outside. This transformation can be observed in process
in the toddler's relationship with his or her teddy bear or Linus
blanket—the so-called *transitional object* (Winnicott, [1951] 1975).

The parents' "Good for you!" which reflected their pleasure in
the child's accomplishments, now is voiced by the part of the self
referred to as the *superego* (Freud, [1923] 1961b), which is com-
posed of both the *ego-ideal* and the *conscience*. Not only does the
superego criticize the self for transgressions, it also praises the self
when the individual lives up to his or her ego-ideal, and it is the
source of a healthy and secure self-esteem. These identifications
with the parents allow the person to do for himself or herself what
once could be done only by parental figures; they are necessary to
the development of full emotional autonomy.

xxxii THE CORE RELATIONSHIP PROBLEM IN PSYCHOTHERAPY

And Now the Eternal Triangle

With the full differentiation of self from object, there is also a firmer differentiation of mother from father. The primary caretaker—mother—is the linchpin of the psyche. Still, there is an attachment to the father even though dependency is vested primarily in the mother. Although the quality of the attachment to the mother as the primary caretaker of infancy is central to the build-up of the earliest self and object representations, an attachment to the father develops as well. Early on he is accepted as a substitute for the absent mother. Then his role becomes increasingly important. He supports individuation from the mother, not only as a substitute for her but also as a provider of different and unique experiences for the developing child. Up to now the child's relationship with each parent has been discrete and dyadic. Now, more and more, the individuality of each parent is recognized and valued differentially. The child becomes aware of the *triangle that includes the self and both mother and father*. The conflict inherent in that triadic relationship emerges. This is the point at which the conflicts of the Oedipus complex (Freud, [1913] 1953c, p. 129) come to the fore. What was a dyadic view of the interpersonal world now must include *two* significant others. A two-way competitiveness within the triangle generates new wishes, anxieties, and defenses. The child wants to be preferred by mother over father and by father over mother. Along with envy, the child now experiences jealousy of a rival who is also loved, and an uncomfortable ambivalence is generated. With patients who complain of the inability to make choices, we may discover that the core relationship conflict originated at this developmental point, where the child expects that to choose one object of the heart's desire is to cause the loss of the other who is equally desired. In some families this expectation may actually be the case; in others it will be only the child's fear or a projection of his or her own jealousy and wish to possess the object.

The relative ease or difficulty of this period will be strongly influenced by prior development and by the nature of the inner, unconscious representational world. The oedipal period tends to overlap with the latter part of the rapprochement phase of the separation-individuation process, so that rapprochement anxieties are aggravated by oedipal strivings. As the child moves closer to father, will mother abandon him or her? The child's ability to negotiate this troublesome period will also be affected by parental attitudes toward the child, who now presents the parents with an increasingly complex little person. The anxiety-generating wishes and feelings of the oedipal period may be repressed, taking their place in the unconscious along with the archaic images of earlier development.

The Unconscious and Psychoanalysis

The consistent and predictable presence of the primary mothering person throughout the early months of life ties the infant's experience together in a particular way. It is through her that the child's body, impulse, feeling, action, and eventually thought become organized as part of the self and integrated not only with each other but also with external reality, of which she is a representative. She is a bridge between the child's inner world of experience and the outer world of reality. Not only does the mothering person mediate the process of organization and of relating to reality but her image is part of what is organized and is the basis for the development of object relatedness as well. Thus her role in the evolution of the self and object representations is critical. When early development within the maternal matrix goes well, the outcome is the achievement of a *cohesive, reality-related, object-related self*.

Character pathology results from failures in this process of organization and may take the form of deficits of cohesion or integration, deficits of reality relatedness, or deficits of object relatedness. With the interruption or distortion of the development of early object relations, the individual does not arrive at a healthy outcome of the separation-individuation process—namely, a well-secured identity, object constancy, and a superego that regulates self-esteem. When structural pathology derives from failures within the relationship sphere in early development, those same core relationship failures will be manifest in here-and-now relationships as well and will be the focus in psychotherapy.

The therapeutic matrix can be viewed as analogous to that provided by the good-enough mother of the early years. It is a relationship within which repair of the defects of character structure, of the unconscious representational world, may take place. In an accepting, understanding, and safe relationship, various split-off aspects of self can be experienced, expressed, and integrated. The therapeutic matrix facilitates the attachment process, which will eventually provide the basis for the internalization of maternal-therapist functions, responses, and interactions, that is, for the further integration of the self within a context of human relatedness. The therapeutic matrix facilitates differentiation, the structuring of the boundaries of the self, the achievement of identity coupled with the achievement of object constancy, and the structuring of a guiding and loving superego. With structural repair and growth, the archaic images of the self and object, which have been playing out in adult interpersonal relationships, will loosen their grip on the individual's life and will fade into the realm of the unconscious.

With a secure sense of identity the adult can explore the repressed, unconscious conflicts of the oedipal period without undue anxiety and thus can finally renounce the wishes of childhood, being free to find suitable adult love objects and to strive for mature goals.

Now that this overview of the stages and processes of early object relations development from a structural perspective has been laid out as a reference point, the following chapters look at some of the specific core relationship problems that may emerge at various places of derailment along this developmental continuum. We always want to know how much healthy development was laid down before the derailment in order to assess the resources and strengths of the individual as well as his or her vulnerabilities. In the event of trauma we need to ask, Who is the child to whom this happened?

How to go about changing our focus from what is structural to what is relational is discussed throughout the chapters in Part One, "The Core Relationship Problem."

Working with the Core Relationship Problem in Psychotherapy

Part One

The Core Relationship Problem

Chapter One

Construction of
the Developmental Hypothesis

The Hypothesis

This chapter is not intended to be nor *could* it be a compendium of what goes into understanding the myriad complexities that characterize any single human being. Rather its goal is to communicate a way of hearing, a way of organizing, *a way of thinking* when we begin our work with a new patient. We wonder to ourselves, How did this person come to be who he or she is at this point in time? How can we understand his or her way of being in the world? In the following chapter, I then discuss a variety of methods for gathering the data we need to make this assessment.

There is no particular magic to arriving at an at least provisional formulation of a core relationship problem. However, it is necessary to have a sound background in infant and childhood development. One cannot leap from doing, say, accounting to doing clinical work based solely on training in a given psychoanalytic theory and technique. If one does not have a background in child psychology (and adolescent psychology), independent study is strongly recommended.

If we know what the minimal requirements are for the child to negotiate successfully the developmental tasks for each successive phase of development from birth on, we can make an assessment as to how closely any given individual's background came to providing those minimal requirements. Where along the developmental continuum did significant problems emerge? Where along this continuum was the child essentially derailed? When we are told of traumatic events that occurred during childhood, we need to ask, Who was the child to whom this happened? Was he or she a relatively healthy child both physically and emotionally? Or was the child already seriously compromised because of preexisting psychological disorder? The psychologically robust child can weather distressing events that the fragile child cannot. The implications for later treatment are important. Do we focus on the trauma and the task of working it through, or do we attend to the underlying character disorder, the structural pathology, as the primary consideration, at least in the early stages of treatment?

The developmental continuum in terms of attachment, separation and individuation, later childhood, and adolescence is described in the Introduction, which gives an overview of the stages of the formative years. It is these stages and processes that we must refer to when we seek to discover the point of emotional and relationship derailment. *What is set up within the interpersonal matrix of the primary relationship becomes structured within the psyche. The self and object representations thus structured and their connecting affect, thoughts, and desires then become manifest later in life interpersonally.* What can be observed in the here and now is a key to the nature of the adult's internal world, which in turn reflects the quality of the relationship milieu within which the baby and small child evolved.

Constitutional Factors

We tend to overlook the constitutional, temperamental givens of the child as contributors to that early relationship milieu. My observation of a number of infants and their subsequent development has brought to my attention the usefulness of Horney's concept of *types* (1945): those who move toward people, those who move away from people, and those who move against people. I have seen these behavioral styles in the very young child when upset: the one who resorts to anxious clinging (toward people), the one who retreats to a distance with the thumb in the mouth (away from people), and the one who may attack the mother, actually hitting out (against people). That these styles affect the mother is certain, not only because they evoke emotions but because of how they are labeled, that is, "demanding," "rejecting," or "bad." These styles may be manifest in the treatment situation, either evoking in the therapist responses similar to those of the mother and thus problematic or enabling in the intuitive and empathic therapist a useful therapeutic attitude and posture. Early infant research (Murphy and Moriarty, 1976) has also revealed innate differences, for example, in reactivity to stimulation and their effects. These researchers noted that "the behavior of the initially active and responsive infant may evoke the mother's repeated efforts to stimulate more responses from him, and a circular pattern of activity leading to further or even more intense activity may result" (p. 81).

In our eagerness to understand the patient in terms of early interpersonal experience, we should not forget about those innate givens that were, and probably still are, part of the mix. Some of these factors may explain why one child out of a malignant family system is able to survive, to leave the family, and to transcend formidable psychological odds, albeit not without the kind of suffering that brings him or her to treatment.

In a review of Sowell's *Late-Talking Children*, psychologist Joseph Adelson (1997) reported the findings that nearly 90 percent of late-talking children are males, that they come from families with a particular cognitive style, and that a majority of the parents are engineers, accountants, computer specialists, and scientists. Many of these children are precocious in music, math, and memory. There seem to be constitutional variations in brain structure itself that predispose individuals to these differences in cognitive learning and functioning. Problems arise on the one hand when these children are misidentified as retarded or autistic because of their late talking, and tragically inappropriate approaches to working with them have been taken. On the other hand parents can become overly invested in the child's precociousness and neglect the emotional side of the child's development. Constitutionally based characteristics can have an impact on the relationship milieu, coming out of the parent's attitude toward those givens.

The First Year and the Capacity for Affect Regulation

Perhaps one of the most important of modern contributions to knowledge about human development at the very start of life is the work of Allan Schore (1996). His integration of the biological with the mental, of neurology with psychology, is a powerful antidote to current trends that eschew psychological concepts and treatment in favor of a purely medical interpretation of and approach to the treatment of psychological disorders. It is also an antidote to postmodern trends that deny the usefulness and even the validity of science. Schore's work powerfully supports concepts of object relations theory, particularly the work of Bowlby (1969) with respect to attachment and Mahler (1968) with respect to the symbiotic phase and subsequent separation and individuation phases of very early development. His work also describes a neurological basis for the failure to develop a cohesive self in the first year of life as described by the self psychologists: it is the result of the failure of the other to function as a *selfobject* (Kohut, 1971). Schore's brilliant linking of a satisfactory negotiation of the early phases with the development of the central nervous system and its implication for later mental and emotional functioning helps us understand, for example, why the devastating effects of a chaotic first year of life cannot be "fixed" simply by a more wholesome experience from that time forward. His observation contains serious implications for the children who have had such unfortunate beginnings and for the adults who adopt them. Prospective adoptive parents should be prepared to deal with these children's residual problems.

Schore particularly attends to the capacity for affect regulation that comes from the satisfactory first year. He writes that "from the moment of birth, the primary caregiver plays an essential role in regulating her infant's psychobiological states, especially disruptions of ongoing states and transitions between states. Because the infant's organ systems (especially its central and peripheral nervous systems) continue to mature over the course of infancy, the caregiver's involvement is critical to processes as basic as the infant's fluid balance regulation and temperature regulation, life-sustaining functions that eventually become autoregulated" (p. 61). And Schore adds that Fogel (1982) "underscored the developmental principle that a major task of the first year is the evolution of affective tolerance for increasingly higher levels of arousal, and that this task is facilitated by the mother's modulation of the infant's highly stimulated states" (p. 62).

Krystal (1978) describes psychic trauma as the outcome of being confronted with *overwhelming* affect. In this situation the "affective responses produce an unbearable psychic state which threatens to disorganize, perhaps even destroy all psychic functions" (p. 82). Elsewhere (Horner, [1979] 1984) I have noted the developmental implications of repeated traumatic states in the first year of life or so.

Khan (1963) referred to *cumulative trauma*, which results when the primary caretaker fails to function adequately as a protective shield for the baby, in a manner that would lead to affect regulation as described by Schore. A nonempathic and nonresponsive mother is not the only problem that may cause this trauma. The child may be ill and in pain that the mother is powerless to alleviate no matter how hard she tries. Whatever the reason, the child is subjected to repeated traumatic states that interfere with the synthesization of a cohesive self. Krystal notes that in adult life the fear of affect may represent a dread of returning to this infantile trauma. Winnicott (1974) views the fear of breakdown in a similar way, a fear that something will happen that indeed has *already* happened. I find it very useful to interpret this fear, and also temporary states of being overwhelmed, as a *memory*, a total recall of something that cannot be remembered in any other way because it never was symbolized by language. Not only does this interpretation separate past from present but it makes an important distinction between the relative helplessness of the baby and the resources that the individual now has as an adult. The child left alone in the crib had to passively endure; the adult does not. Furthermore, the emergence of the traumatic state no longer signifies to the patient that he or she is "crazy" or hopelessly mentally ill. To understand the state as a *remembering* is not only far less damaging to the patient's self-esteem and to his or her self-image but also leads to a more optimistic attitude on the part of the patient (and perhaps on the part of the therapist as well).

Lachmann and Beebe (1996b) note organizing principles that describe how interactions in the first year of life are regulated, represented, and begin to be internalized: "The principles are *ongoing regulations*, *disruption and repair* of ongoing regulations, and *heightened affective moments*. They further define the nature of self- and mutual regulation. They constitute hypotheses about how social interactions become patterned and salient in the first year." And, importantly, Lachmann and Beebe "propose that these patterns are applicable through metaphor and analogy to the patterning of analyst-patient interactions" (p. 1). Also, "in adults, the capacity for symbolization and the subjective elaboration of experience in the form of fantasies, wishes, and defenses further modifies the organization and representation of interactive patterns" (p. 3). The key words in their description of this process are *dyadic* and *interactive*, that is, relational.

Clinical Manifestations of Early Derailment

Under the heading core relationship problem, we will find issues of very early developmental failure and deficit or issues of somewhat later emerging conflict. Self psychologists pay special attention to deficits of the self. A core relationship *failure* refers to this situation. A core relationship *conflict* evolves further along the developmental continuum, perhaps as the child strives for autonomy. Relationship, however, is still the operative word. The earlier the core relationship problem develops, the more disordered the organization of the self, whether it be a chaotic disorganization under stress or a paranoid organization that resulted because the infant's world consisted of interactions with a frightening, hurtful caretaker alternating with times of aloneness and abandonment that led to anaclitic depression. Defenses against these dangers such as schizoid detachment and also compensatory mechanisms such as reliance upon the intellect will be evident in the individual's way of being in the world. Later on we may find this individual clinging to persecutory relationships internal or external in preference to experiencing the black hole (Grotstein, 1990) or the empty despair of the anaclitic depression. Any object is better than no object.

When someone tells us at the start of treatment that he feels that he is dead, that he died a long time ago, and that he is not capable of attachment or love, that the only attachment he has is to his depression, we need to think about these findings with respect to development in the first year of life. We may hypothesize that the failure of maternal responsiveness left him in a chronic state of anaclitic depression, or we may hypothesize that because of the mother's depression, the only connection between them was their joining in this affective state, or we may hypothesize that both these problems coexist. For him, depression may signify both object loss and object connection. We know we have to connect with him in that uncomfortable place because if we respond to our own discomfort with attempts to make him feel better, with medication or otherwise, we will leave him as alone as he was as an infant. This situation is discussed further in Chapter Fifteen in examining the negative therapeutic reaction.

When someone else tells us that she does not know who she is if she is not in a relationship, that she does not know who she is supposed to be, once again we can think about failures of her caretakers to connect in the ways described by Schore or by Lachmann and Beebe, and this informs us of what is needed in the treatment relationship.

We can also consider Winnicott's concept ([1962] 1965b) of the *true/false self split*, where connection is possible only through the adaptations demanded by the primary caretakers. The more pervasive and the earlier the demand for adaptation to the emotional needs of the other and for the suppression and repression of the self, the more primitive will the true self seem when it emerges in the course of therapy. Attempts to bypass these core relationship problems will lead to early failure of the treatment, repeating the early traumatic failures of the primary caretakers. Winnicott ([1960] 1965a) writes: "In psycho-analytic work it is possible to see analyses going on indefinitely because they are done on the basis of work with the False Self. . . . A principle may be enunciated, that in the False Self area of our analytic practice we find we make more headway by recognition of the patient's non-existence than by a long-continued working with the patient on the basis of ego-defence mechanisms" (pp. 151–152).

So what data do we look for at the start of the treatment process to help us set up our developmental hypothesis in terms of the core relationship problem? Some specific guidelines are discussed in the next chapter.

Chapter Two

Construction of the Developmental Hypothesis

Method of Data Gathering

Once we have alerted ourselves to the importance of identifying the core relationship problem, we may wonder how we can get the data that will tell us whether or not the patient's first year was spent in an *average expectable environment*, that is, one with the kind of caregiving that ensures the ability to tolerate and successfully deal with strong emotion. The work of Schore and of Lachmann and Beebe with respect to this earliest development was discussed in the preceding chapter. Certainly, the patient will not have direct memory to report, but there are data that will provide clues.

For example, the patient may tell us she is the fourth child of seven, that they all were eighteen months to two years apart, and that the mother was the only caregiver. Not only was the mother probably frequently distraught or unavailable, the chaos and even assaultiveness of the sibling milieu would lead to trauma and either chronic breakdown or defensive detachment. We can at least hypothesize that development in the most critical years was at best seriously deficient if not disastrously compromised. Of course we will also want to look for and understand the individual's strengths, the compensatory or defensive mechanisms or strategies that enable the person to function at a higher level than the far less than optimal beginning might suggest.

Kohut (1977) calls our attention to the distinction between *primary structures*, which arise out of the earliest relationship with the mother, and later *defensive*, *secondary*, or *compensatory* structures, which may arise out of other important relationships, especially with the father or as ways to defend against the distress of the primary relationship setup. It will be important to know what these structures are, to understand the complexities of the individual's way of being in the world, to know where there is vulnerability, and to know where there is strength. Bromberg (1980) speaks of the importance of knowing where the patient is on the *empathy-anxiety gradient* at any given moment in the treatment situation. We have to know when to function as a selfobject and when to interpret conflict.

Other data also enable us to generate hypotheses, which, of course, we will constantly be testing and amending as new information emerges in the treatment situation, especially the subtle or not-so-subtle interaction of transference and countertransference. This chapter describes a number of issues that emerge within the clinical relationship and that can function as important information sources: transference resistance, family structure, the earliest memory, intake interview issues, special meanings of patient communications, and the presenting symptom.

Transference Resistance

Transference resistance is a defensive mode of relating to the therapist. It can be viewed as the patient's way of *managing* the therapeutic relationship to bring about a kind of interaction that is wished-for or to prevent a kind of interaction that is feared and a source of anxiety. It may come out of anxiety due to a neurotic conflict. It may also be based on the dictates of character pathology.

Friedman (1997) refers to the *demand structure of the treatment*, observing that "if you don't offer one demand, the patient will perceive another" (p. 29). The perceived demand will derive from conscious or unconscious expectations inherent in the core relationship problem. Examples of therapist demands that patients assume are that the patient must be responsive to the therapist's assumed narcissistic vulnerabilities, that she must never upset the therapist, and that the therapist's love must be bought at a price to the self. The patient will relate to the therapist in adaptation to these perceived demands. These ways of being with the therapist are examples of transference resistance.

Attending to the transference resistance gives direct information about the wishes and fears associated with the core relationship problem, or conflict. It also provides information with respect to the adaptations and defenses that have evolved over the years and that now cause problems themselves. That is, they are maladaptive even though they may have felt necessary at one time to the survival of the self. Transference resistance is often central to the therapeutic impasse and often requires the therapist's conscious or unconscious collusion.

Playing the role of *good patient* is a frequent manifestation of this dynamic. The word resistance applies because the adaptation blocks the kind of work necessary to reach the therapeutic goal. An individual who brings in dreams but clearly shows no interest in understanding them may well be complying with what that individual assumes is desired of him. If the therapist takes full responsibility for interpreting the dream without requiring that the patient work with her by providing associations, she is colluding with the charade. In cases such as this the interpretations will go in one ear and out the other.

Paying close attention to the transference-countertransference mix, we want to know how the patient attempts to connect with us as it may reveal both a wish to connect and a posture that defends against the felt dangers of the very connection the patient wishes for. What is evoked in us that is resonating with such a complex of embedded wish and defense? For example, if the person tries to figure out what we want so that she can provide it, we may feel strangely alone or even sleepy. It does not feel as if we are engaged with a living person. This kind of automatic shifting in adaptation to the assumed needs of the other also reveals an assumption about the character of the therapist; like the mother, the therapist is assumed to be an infantile narcissistic individual who must be catered to if the patient is to be safe. Exploring the typical or perhaps even several typical strategies the person uses to try to connect provides important information about the early relationship setup as well as about the coping strategies developed to deal with the conflicts inherent in the setup.

Does the person alternate between intense attempts to *connect* (through seduction or ingratiation or self-effacing servitude) and to *take flight away from relationship* in order to reconnect with the self? A history of an in-and-out pattern of therapy may indicate the existence of a *double approach-avoidance* relationship conflict. To connect with the other is to lose the self. To connect with the self is to lose the other. This kind of vacillation in and out of relationship will characterize the person's way of being in the world. The person will be hopeless that relationships can ever work out.

Once we have ascertained the core relationship conflict as it is manifest in the treatment relationship, it is important that it be laid out in a manner that communicates empathy. In the case of the double approach-avoidance in this example, the therapist can communicate empathy with the lose-lose aspect of the person's dilemma. The sooner this core relationship conflict is interpreted, the less likely the patient is to act out against the therapist and the therapy.

The Family Structure

Birth order and the role of siblings is given short shrift in psychoanalytic theory. I have found many, many times that the birth of a second child is far more traumatic for the firstborn than is often recognized. We are familiar with the concept of sibling rivalry. Even more important is the degree to which the birth of the new baby may constitute a severe narcissistic wound for the firstborn, who heretofore experienced the specialness attendant on being, at least for a time, the only child. Sometimes, paradoxically, the better the relationship with the mother in the first years, the greater the felt betrayal and the greater the wound. The two- or three-year-old is likely to try to explain to himself why he was "not enough," in some cases developing strategies to make himself important to his mother again. Such strategies tend to be adaptive or compliant leading to a splitting off of the abandoned and angry true self. This is another example of how we look to the past to understand where optimal development was compromised or derailed by life circumstances alone. We cannot leap to the conclusion that there was a bad mother even though from the very small child's point of view she failed to be what the child needed. The splitting off and repression of the hurt and angry three-year-old does not have the same implications for treatment as a more primitive splitting, or more precisely, a failure of integration. Despite unresolved dependency issues vis-à-vis the mother who disappointed, the analytic work in these cases can rely on an observing ego, a cohesive self, a reliable therapeutic alliance, and despite transference resistance, an absence of primitive enactments.

Sibling jealousies and rivalries may become manifest when the issue of having children of one's own comes to the fore for the adult. The marital dyad, with its many transference possibilities, may be stressed at the prospect of an infant who poses a threat to the exclusivity of that dyad. I have heard fathers who had to overcome an initial hatred of their own child. One man was remembered as having been so furious at the age of three when he observed his mother nursing the new baby that she had to discontinue the breast feeding. Allison (1997) describes psychogenic infertility as the outcome of intense repressed sibling rivalry.

We may hear information that alerts us to significant core pathology when the patient's family was chaotic, with several poorly cared-for children essentially fending for themselves, an alcoholic mother, and battling parents. We can expect that external chaos to be mirrored in the internal chaos at the core of the person's personality. We will look for the kinds of defenses and adaptations that enabled the person to survive the family milieu but should not underestimate the core weakness even in the face of apparently successful later adaptation.

The Earliest Memory

Asking for the individual's earliest memory frequently provides an important key to a core problem. It is often a wonderful metaphor for this problem and can be referred to when the problem comes up, as it will, again and again in the course of treatment. A memory of being left at home with an earache, crying because the rest of the family went on a picnic, can signify pain at early abandonments. It might also suggest a readiness to experience psychic pain through somatic manifestations, as discussed in Chapter One. The power and persistence of the earliest memory often comes as much from what it came to mean and how it became an organizer for later experiences as from the actual trauma of the moment.

Equally significant information can come from fond memories, such as the memory of making cookies with a grandmother who died when the patient was young, a memory that would come to signify the wished-for and lost good object, whether the mother of infancy or the grandmother herself. We also may come to understand from a positive memory like this a dilemma for the individual such as having been caught in a triangle with the loved grandmother and the mother who was jealous of their relationship, and we may learn the power of that triangle and its manifestations in later situations that replicated the setup over and over. We may learn that as an adult the individual tends to have an unsatisfactory, ongoing primary relationship and at the same time finds grandmother substitutes in one form or another, these often being interchangeable. These situations will not be oedipal triangles although they might be misunderstood by the therapist as such.

The therapist may be puzzled to find that what was a very positive initial transference (grandmother transference) changes abruptly when some perceived failure of the therapist leads to a shift to the negative mother transference. As much as it might look the same, this situation is different in important ways from the classical split within the character structure of the narcissistic personality disorder as described by Kohut (1971). The earliest memory will be the key to this acting-out dynamic, both in and out of the treatment situation.

The earliest memory may give us insight into what appear to be here-and-now anxieties of a specific kind. Remembering the terror of being lost in a department store at the age of three may relate to panic felt when driving in unfamiliar locations where the fear of getting lost is incompatible with the characteristic high level of functioning in other emergency situations. Despite the anxiety, there is a cohesive self, and the patient can tolerate the anxiety and work interpretively. The metaphor of being lost will help unravel later emotional elaborations of the fear and defenses against it. Perhaps getting lost (emotionally abandoned) will be the consequence of moves toward autonomy.

End-of-the-hour comments such as "there's never enough time" may signify, for example, a mother who could not tolerate the regression of refueling during the rapprochement period or, even after that, a mother who demanded from the child a self-sufficiency of which she was not yet capable. The core relationship conflict will be around the need to perform—to be a big girl—with denial of dependency wishes and an avoidance of that aspect of the transference and of the analytic work as well. To complicate this scenario, shame becomes associated with the baby self and pride with the ability to perform. Shame-pride issues often complicate relationship conflict. Sometimes this developmental background becomes manifest in what is referred to as a *resistance to a dependent transference*. This is a particular variety of transference resistance.

Intake Interview Issues

Of course the intake interview at the very start of treatment seeks to elicit information about both the person's present day life and family and developmental history as the person recalls it. Questions can be formulated to evoke relationship data and to see if patterns readily emerge, which they often do. Specific questions about the way the individual related to mother, to father, and to little brother and how other family members related to one another fill out the picture. Again it is a matter of how one listens and synthesizes that may render the intake either dry and unproductive or rich in clues about the core relationship conflict, how it arose, and what its psychological consequences have been throughout life. A willingness to wander about in the interview, to clarify and inquire when it makes sense, can make even a somewhat formal interview rich in what is gleaned from it.

For example, in her first session a woman commented on her terrible guilt. I asked, "So what's your crime?" Without hesitation she replied, "To have a self." These four words opened up the exploration of both inner and interpersonal consequences of her having been abused emotionally and physically, with a constant assault on anything that might be deemed expressive of self. If she failed to hide her feelings, she felt the back of her father's hand. If she expressed her thoughts, she was told she was crazy. If she expressed wish or need, she was told she was selfish.

The Structure of Therapy and Evidence of the Core Relationship Problem

Bromberg (1996a) notes that we do not try to cure people of what happened to them. We try to cure them of what they now do to themselves and others in order to cope with what happened to them. From these maladaptive patterns of life we will be able to pull out the underlying wishes and fears with respect to relationships.

Some patients are so distraught at the first meeting that a formal inquiry is not possible. Nevertheless, if one's ear is attuned to the meaning of the patient's communications, much can be learned, to be perhaps put aside for the moment but brought forth at a later time when it is clinically appropriate. As always in doing the work of the psychotherapist—whatever you may have learned in your studies, from supervisors, or from books such as this one—ultimately, it will be your sensitivity, your tact, your interpersonal skill that will make the application of such information helpful or not.

How the therapy structure is set up with respect to frequency of meetings and paying of fees will also be rich in clinically relevant information. If the patient wants to come in only once a week but submits to the therapist's insistence that it must be more in order that the work be productive, the therapist may find that she has inadvertently activated a core conflict characterized by a pattern of overt compliance and covert defiance that simultaneously connects and distances the person from the other. There is a wish *and* a fear with respect to intimate relationships.

When did this conflict begin and what was the relationship milieu in which it developed? In a situation like this the therapist may inadvertently take on the role of container of the wish or desire, which allows the patient to deny his own wish, quite probably replicating an early demand that he take care of his mother and give in to her needs and demands. The patient does not have to experience the wish-fear conflict within himself if he is able to get the other person to be a proxy for one side of the conflict. The therapist's stance of neutrality toward the conflicting forces will prevent this externalization of intrapsychic conflict. If this externalization does take place, the conflict will appear to be between patient and therapist and may be seen as a power struggle.

Should the therapist, with or without the help of consultation, catch on that this is what has happened, a direct discussion about it, including the therapist's role, can free up the work. The relevance to the early pattern with the mother and the characterological adaptations to the conflict can be interpreted and eventually worked through. This type of clinical impasse can be activated when the patient misses sessions and the therapist calls to see what the problem is and to wonder when the person will return. Such follow-up may be appropriate under certain circumstances, when a patient is deemed suicidal for example. However, especially when the therapist is concerned about losing a patient, the therapist may be perceived as the one who needs to meet rather than the patient. Here too the therapist becomes the holder of the desire while the patient can deny his own. In contrast, communicating, "I will be here when *you* want to come in," puts the ball in the patient's court, so to speak. He has to acknowledge his own wishes and needs rather than attributing them to the therapist. It will also feel like a replication of the relationship with his mother in which her needs and wishes always seemed to take precedence over his. Distancing defenses if not outright quitting of treatment may be activated in the service of maintaining boundaries or autonomy but at the cost of getting help.

However, Lachmann (Lachmann and Beebe, 1996a) describes a situation in which reminder calls to the patient served to let her know that she was wanted, and he reports a line in a poem she had written that said, "Run after me but never let me go." He notes that whatever role his own anxiety played in the decision to make the calls, from her perspective they were crucial to the work. As in every situation, we cannot look to general rules to guide our clinical decisions. The decision to call or not to call has to come from our understanding of what each choice would mean to the patient in terms of that patient's own core problems.

The Presenting Symptom

A man troubled by his compulsive cross-dressing made it clear that his desire was toward women. However, it was felt as coming from himself as a woman. He joked about being a male lesbian. He emphasized that he was not a transsexual. He almost boasted that he could get any woman he wanted, that he could get inside her and conquer her. He also commented that he felt like a little boy and had sex with women to find out what it was like to be a man.

The patient's father had deserted the family when the patient was ten years old, leaving him in the care of his angry, possessive, and controlling mother and two aunts. The mother was angry when he married and pleased when he divorced. She called him every day. As he was growing up she was overprotective, decided everything for him and figured everything out for him. He commented that if he could remain a child or be a girl, everything would be OK.

The core relationship conflict revolved around his mother's need to keep him dependent on her and her wish that he had been a girl. He grew up terrified of losing her and made the necessary adaptations that would ensure her continuing attachment to him. Despite his renunciation of gender to please her, his sense of biological maleness was intact, quite probably due to the early influence of the father. His renunciation of adult status was also in the service of preventing her abandonment of him. The core relationship problem entailed the many aspects of individuation that were blocked by his mother and were to become the focus of treatment. His problem had nothing to do with sex, although it was played out in the sexual arena. His need to get inside a woman to conquer her reflected the insecurity of his attachment to his mother.

The core relationship problem is essentially the scaffold around which subsequent development is organized, and it has complex paths leading from it in many directions. Construction of the developmental hypothesis is not the end of the work: it is the start. Understanding where the child was developmentally when the conflict arose also tells us what strengths and vulnerabilities existed at the time of the derailment. Was he a toddler with limited language abilities, or was he just starting school? What were the child's abilities to reason and to process his own experience? Was he still prone to magical thinking? Did he think concretely or could he understand cause and effect? This is where background knowledge about overall child development is important for a therapist.

The therapist has to be something of a novelist, able to put together the person's story (for "history" read "his story") from a wide variety of the person's informative communications. The story provides a matrix within which the patient can be better understood in the here and now, so that ultimately everything that transpires in the course of treatment makes sense. That which the patient fears is "crazy" can come to be seen as understandable under the circumstances. That alone relieves the individual of shame and anxiety about his life, about who he is in the world today.

As we listen to the patient in our ongoing data-gathering process *throughout* treatment, we may fail to pay close enough attention to words spoken by the patient whose meaning seems obvious to us. If we are alert to the importance of understanding the patient's personal and idiosyncratic meanings and associations linked to everyday words, especially words that define or describe, we will stop and wonder with the patient what a specific word signifies to him or to her. We will often be surprised at how far off we were in our assumptions and at how productive the exploration of the patient's meanings is for the treatment. The next chapter specifically addresses the topic of the signifier.

Chapter Three

The Place of the Signifier in Psychoanalytic Object Relations Theory

Noting that the unconscious is a symbol-forming organ, Lacan points out that meaning is created at every level of the mind. A *signifier* is a symbol, standing as it does for something else. Lacan assumes that chains of signifiers connect through associations rather than the laws of syntax. And he tells us that there is no meaning except that which we structure within the chain of signifiers (Van Buren, 1993). This chapter addresses how we listen for the patient's meanings.

The Lacanian attention to words as signifiers and to their place in the association process that leads to the formation of meaning reminds us of the value of free association in the analytic method. Makari and Shapiro (1993) take note of what they call the *linguistic turn* in psychoanalysis. They write: "In so privileging language, Lacan concluded that the analyst must attend to the details and nuances of words themselves. Lacan [called] this process the play of signifiers, for it was in this assortment of signifiers . . . that one found unconsciously encoded messages. Lacan understood repression to be the block between a signifier and what it truly signified" (p. 997).

The build-up of internal object relations, of self and object representations in affectively charged and dynamic relation to one

The author gratefully acknowledges permission to reprint this article, with slight adaptations, which was originally published in the *Journal of the American Academy of Psychoanalysts*, 1995, *23*, 71–78. Copyright © 1995 by The American Academy of Psychoanalysis.

another, is mediated by the meanings the child comes to attribute to its experiences of self in the world. We are meaning-making animals, and willy-nilly, the child *will* create meaning from his or her earliest times of mental organization.

If we think of the self and object representations as signifiers, we do not stop at the level of developmental and structural diagnosis but seek to discover with the patient the historically built up network of meanings that contributes to the complexity and richness of the signifiers self and object. In effect we all speak a kind of shorthand, and only our genuine interest in the other's meanings will enable us to see and hear beyond what presents as the obvious. Associations spread out not only horizontally but vertically as well.

Lacan's concept of *desire* as the wish for the primary object, or desire for the other, stands as a comfortable connection between Lacan and object relations thinking. Indeed, his concept of desire reminds us of Fairbairn's dictum that the infant is object seeking and not gratification seeking. At the same time, other concepts concerning the presymbolic level of infantile experience are consistent with Mahler's idea of a normal stage of autism at the beginning of life. For example, Kristeva (1982) conceptualizes the mother's function as helping the infant form images out of the void. This view is also consistent with Mahler's formulations. Van Buren (1993) writes, "It seems to me that the journey from archaic, preverbal states to representations at the level of the symbolic, in which one object stands for another, yielding the meanings that express the experience of the 'I,' is the quintessential hallmark of subjectivity." One might add that this journey yields the meanings that express the experience of the "other" as well. Van Buren goes on to say that "meaning accrues at each level from the somatic to abstract representations, or from the formless infinite . . . to graspable meaning" (p. 578).

Lacan, Kristeva, and others who look at the emergence of language and meaning explicate the mental process through which the internal world of object relations comes into being. As theoretical viewpoints, their ideas enhance one another.

Intuitive Listening

The task of accessing meaning from the patient's associations requires an intuitive listening. Samuel Taylor Coleridge wrote of poetic perception that

> *The poet in his lone yet genial hour*
> *Gives to his eyes a magnifying power:*
> *Or rather he emancipates his eyes*
> *From the black shapeless accidents of size—*
> *In unctuous cones of kindling coal,*
> *Or smoke upwreathing from the pipe's trim bole,*
> > *His gifted ken can see*
> > *Phantoms of sublimity.*

Each person who comes to us to be seen, to be heard, to be found, so that ultimately he can find himself, presents that self much as a poet presents a poem. We, as patient reader, let his poetry wash over our receptive consciousness, to hear the many levels of meaning, of condensation and paradox, of image and of metaphor. But listen as we may, we will need his help that we may understand his poem as he has written it. It is not our theoretical sophistication that will help us enter his world of meaning, to follow the flowing threads of his signifiers as they carry us to the essence of who he is. Leavy (1993), discussing "self and sign in free association," says that the analytic setting in which free association is paramount permits the disclosure of the lived self.

In the thirteenth century a volume of Jewish visionary lore was published. Entitled *The Zohar: The Book of Splendor* (see Hoffman, 1989), it contained a blend of metaphysics, mystical cosmogony, and esoteric psychology. It focused on the hidden meaning of biblical stories and said, "Woe unto those who see in the Law nothing but simple narratives and ordinary words" (pp. 16–17). Woe unto the therapist who hears only simple narratives and ordinary words—and we might add, to his or her patient as well.

I do not see the role of the therapist as a passive one in the search for the patient's meanings. The association process may yield to discovery when it is not totally free. An "I'm not completely sure what that word means for you" leads the patient in the direction of her own association chains and thus to the mother lode contained in the signifier.

Let us say a patient comes in and reports being able to recall only a fragment of a dream. In it, you and the patient are sitting at the breakfast table. Why is the breakfast table in the dream? What wealth of memory, association, and meaning is contained in the concrete furniture of the dream scene? If we are not attuned to the importance of the role of the signifier, assuming too readily that we know what the patient is talking about, we will not make those necessary inquiries that open the door to an underground cavern and its treasures and demons. Leavy (1993) agrees when he writes that "the capacity of the analysts to empathize is a talent for recognizing kindred experiences in their own network of signifiers. . . . Its pertinence springs from the reality that analyst and patient use a shared language, bearing networks of signifiers that are literally 'familiar.' It ought to be the opposite of imposing theory on patients; it enables analysts to *ask questions that lead to the progressive unconcealing of meaning*" (p. 417, emphasis added).

When we are not able to comprehend the implications of the signifier directly, asking what is the opposite of the word in question may uncover the conflict embedded in the meaning. With a smile, a young woman informed me she was becoming "decadent." I asked for clarification, and as examples she gave me sitting in the sun, listening to Mozart, and reading a novel. In my lexicon these behaviors hardly qualify as decadent. I asked her what the opposite of decadent was, and without hesitation she replied, "rigidly moral." Although this conflict was manifest in her expectation that I would be critical of her, the further relevance of being rigidly moral to her anxieties and defenses could now be explored. The word yes is devoid of its assumed meaning if the individual does not have the word no in her volitional and communication repertoires.

To the people I supervise, I often have to say again and again: "Inquire. Inquire. Inquire."

Theory Versus Strategy

Theories as ways of organizing data should be distinguished from methods or strategies as tactics for gathering data. The search for the patient's meaning is important as a strategy for gathering data that provide the wherewithal for theory construction, but it is also important as a therapeutic instrument in and of itself. Whether the focus is on empathy or on meaning, tactics that search for meaning are critical for the analytic practitioner regardless of his or her preferred theory. There is nothing incompatible between a theory of psychic structure and a collaborative search for the patient's system of meanings.

The more attention I pay to the complexities of the patient's signifiers, the better I am able to perceive internal organization of meaning, belief, affect, and action in object relations terms. I think it is a serious mistake to become so enamored of postmodern ideas that we throw out the very notion of theory and what it has to offer. In my experience the appropriate clinical use of theoretical concepts and attention to meaning potentiate one another. Interpretations made in the context of the patient's meanings have the ring of truth for the patient. Leavy (1993), who sees free association and through it the *recovery* of the self as common to all psychoanalytic theories, writes that for him, "a longtime expositor of psychoanalysis as a process of dialogue, the work of theory in our field is to lay hold of the unconcealing of the self that takes place in the speech of our patients, and to wrestle with our discoveries" (p. 421).

The self has been a central concept for humanistic-existential thinkers and therapists for generations. Summarizing Buber, Friedman (1994) writes that "the inmost growth of the self is not accomplished by our relation to ourselves, but by the confirmation in which one knows oneself to be made present in one's uniqueness by another. Self-realization and self-actualization, from this standpoint, are not the goal but the by-product. The process relies on mutual confirmation, cooperation, and genuine dialogue" (p. 58).

With the growing focus on the self in psychoanalytic theory and technique, psychoanalysis comes ever closer to the humanistic perspective. And indeed, its goal is a humanistic one. The difference between them becomes increasingly theoretical, that is, it rests on the way in which data are systematically organized in the mind of the analyst. If psychoanalysis dispenses with theory, that distinction will be lost and with it the fabric of psychoanalytic identity. Even more important, the greater technical skills that come with that understanding will be lost. Buber is an interpersonal psychoanalyst without the theory.

Story of an Empty Space

In thinking about the intransigence of certain symptomatic experiences, it seems to me that even when we interpret dynamics correctly, we may miss the emotional hold the symptom has because of its complexities as a signifier. I have in mind a woman who suffered from a sense of what she called an "empty place" in her, and her lifelong futile attempts to "fill it" with a certain kind of relationship. Exploration revealed that the empty space was not the black hole described by Grotstein (1990) and alluded to by Winnicott ([1962] 1965b) when he spoke of "unthinkable anxiety," such as a feeling of falling forever, going to pieces, having no relation to one's body, or having no orientation. He refers to these fears as *psychotic anxieties*, although he views them also as a normal aspect of very early life. In a similar vein, Kristeva (1982) writes of the abyss of meaninglessness that she designates the *abject*. It is the role of the mother to soothe and contain her baby so as to alleviate these primitive terrors.

The empty space described by this patient seemed to have its own shape and, although painful, was endurable. After I worked with her for several years on her acting out inside and outside of the treatment situation, work leading to significant behavioral and attitudinal changes in her interpersonal relationships, it occurred to me that the empty space *was* her object representation. Of course it could never be filled, as it was not a space at all. To her it signified the sense of something missing (her unavailable mother) and the feelings of yearning that actually connected her to the absent mother. Her way of being in the world came to be characterized by adaptation to the needs of the other in a completely self-effacing manner. Although this adaptation protected her from feeling the pain and anxiety of frustrated yearning, it led to an alienation from her sense of who she was.

In the end, of course, this adaptation increased her felt dependency on others and intensified her underlying anxiety. Treatment would not change the early self and object setup that was characterized by the signifier empty space, but with the therapist as a new object who did not require self-annihilation from her, she was no longer alone with the pain as she had been as a small and helpless child. Furthermore, she was able to integrate her own strengths and resources, which decreased her sense of helplessness and dependency. And this development decreased the basic anxiety that she had defended against all her life. The empty space became a slight and poignant ache, and she was comfortable with it as a connection to her internal object.

However, it was not until she and I came to understand what the empty space signified that behavioral and attitudinal changes could be consolidated. No longer would they evoke the anxiety of abandonment. In fact the respect she now found accorded her in the world at large gave her a new source of self-esteem, as this respect mirrored parts of herself that had remained hidden for so long.

I think the empty space as signifier stood not only for the totality of her experience with her early mother but also for the sense of self that was linked to the mother through the longing. In a black hole experience, there is a terrifying sense of self-annihilation and nothingness. That was not true of this patient's empty space experience. The tie with the concepts of structural internal representations is evident. Her beliefs about herself and about others as well as her beliefs about what relationships were like came to elaborate the core problem. Her later relationship with her mother reinforced the early experience by virtue of the mother's narcissistic deafness and blindness to who her daughter was. The word mother came to signify the mother of later consciousness, whereas empty space signified the preverbal representation.

The Significance of Language

In the clinical situation, as much as we of necessity use words to articulate experience, thought, feeling, or belief, the words we choose may take on a life of their own and lock us into a limited or inaccurate position. The word, intended as a signifier, becomes the thing. For example, if we chose to describe something that is going on in the treatment relationship as a "power struggle" from the patient's viewpoint, those words may orient us in a direction best not taken. Once we have used those words, our own power issues may be activated in the countertransference, even though we may think we have a good handle on them.

The words we choose may cause an unconscious countertransference reaction as well. On the one hand, putting certain words, such as power struggle, out to the patient may evoke in him a defensive posture that is not clinically useful. If on the other hand we say that the individual's sense of safety seems to be dependent on his ability to feel in control, our own internal workings take us in a different direction. If I know the individual is frightened at the prospect of not being in control in the interpersonal situation, my empathy and my intellect can be used in the service of helping him with the underlying fear. Perhaps exploring the need-fear dilemma in terms of the core relationship conflict, along with the defenses that have been built up in order to cope with the attendant, guilt, anxiety, or depression, can lead to an interpretation that will make the person feel less endangered—and thus less need to control.

Shawver (forthcoming) discusses new ways to think about how language affects our understanding. Working from a postmodern perspective, she notes that "language passages all have an implicit layer of metaphor and parable that tend to 'enchant' us because, in order to understand what is being said, we suspend our appreciation of other points of view." She notes how hidden metaphors can shape the way we relate to problems. Certainly our use of the phrase power struggle will shape the way we relate to the patient. Shawver describes the effect of switching metaphors, such as changing "childish" to "youthful," showing how this switch brings in a completely new arena of signification. Others have referred to this switch as *reframing*. Shawver likes the term *transvaluation*. She cites Ingram (1996), who reframed a patient's self-concept from "a trouble-maker" to "a maverick." This reframing is all well and good, but we have to be careful not to impose our own preferred transvaluation on what the person is trying to tell us. First, I would want to know what trouble-maker signifies to the patient in relationship terms. Does it imply that the patient's very existence is deemed antithetical to the well-being of the object? The consequences of this belief may well describe the rest of his psychic and interpersonal life! Perhaps eventually the more positive and self-enhancing articulation or expression of self can be used as a new, now conflict-free appellation.

Other words some patients use in self-description are equally pejorative, distracting attention from the underlying interpersonal anxieties. "I'm a procrastinator" or "I'm just lazy" fails to address the underlying avoidance defenses against anxiety-provoking interpersonal situations.

We may tend to become enchanted by a particular way of viewing things when we need to be free to choose from outside that perspective. Theoretical constructs can sometimes enchant us in this way. Postmodern concepts about attending carefully to words, to hidden metaphors and parables, or to implicit beliefs introduce an orientation toward both listening and speaking that opens up possibilities both in and out of the clinical situation.

How the Therapist Becomes a Signifier

Concepts associated with postmodernism are not necessarily anti-thetical to a structural point of view. They remind us that although our structural concepts are as useful to us as the study of anatomy is to the nascent physician, they are not the whole story. When we think of any given patient, his or her name will stand as a signifier for us of the total experience of the person, and although we may stand back and articulate a structural diagnosis, that can never be the defining aspect of the therapeutic relationship. Ingram (1993) refers to the *signature* of that relationship, its unique and unrepro-ducible quality. If we are not comfortable with this level of *being with* the person, we are in danger of becoming either automatons or doctrinaire practitioners. However we are, we will ultimately be-come a signifier for the patient that will encompass far more than our empathy or our interpretations.

E. E. Cummings intuited this wisdom when he wrote:

> *one winter afternoon*
>
> *(at the magical hour*
> *when is becomes if)*
>
> *a bespangled clown*
> *standing on eighth street*
> *handed me a flower.*
>
> *Nobody,it's safe*
> *to say,observed him but*
>
> *myself;and why?because*
>
> *without any doubt he was*
> *whatever(first and last)*

mostpeople fear most;
a mystery for which i've
no word except alive

—that is,completely alert
and miraculously whole;

with not merely a mind and a heart

but unquestionably a soul—
by no means funereally hilarious

(or otherwise democratic)
but essentially poetic
or ethereally serious:

a fine not a coarse clown
(no mob,but a person)

and while never saying a word

who was anything but dumb;
since the silence of him

self sang like a bird.
Mostpeople have been heard
screaming for international

measures that render hell rational
—i thank heaven somebody's crazy

enough to give me a daisy

Though the focus of this book thus far has been on the individual and his or her developmental conflicts and the words he or she uses to communicate them, we have to keep in mind that the child is affected in many ways by the family milieu and relationships within which the child develops. One major cause of psychological derailment is a pathological family system within which the small child becomes embroiled. The child's adaptations to that system often constitute the core relationship problem with which we will be concerned in treatment. Familiarity with family systems concepts is a sine qua non for the therapist if he or she is to be effective in working with the patient for whom this is a major factor. In the next chapter certain systems-related pathology is discussed.

Chapter Four

The Contribution of Family System Pathology to Core Relationship Problems

In Chapter Two, I wrote that the core relationship conflict is essentially the scaffold around which subsequent development is organized and that it has complex paths leading from it in many directions. Construction of the developmental hypothesis is not the end of the work: it is the start. Moreover, subsequent developmental complexities may have to be attended to first, especially when they are derived from a pathological family system. This chapter discusses some problem dynamics of the pathological family system: the double-bind on achievement, projective identification, and various modes of binding. When the child is taken up into parental fantasies and projections, the sense of self in relation to the other will be the outcome of the kinds of adaptations the child had to make, both interpersonally and intrapsychically. However, the point of the original derailment is still relevant when it comes time to attend to the emergent true self. The point of the original derailment will also tell us about the basic strengths and vulnerabilities we can expect or rely on in our clinical work with the individual.

Until recently, the psychoanalytic literature has been sparse with respect to the contribution of family system pathology to psychopathology of later life. A notable exception has been Slipp (1984), who described in an earlier article (1973) what he calls the *symbiotic survival pattern*, in which one individual is made responsible for the self-esteem or survival of another member.

Calogeras and Alston (1985) wrote about the relationship between family pathology and the infantile neurosis. They describe the situation in which the pathological family milieu succeeds in providing a certain *critical state* for the maintenance of the childhood in adulthood, and how it is a major inhibiting force in the failure to resolve the pathology. It is important for the therapist who works with the psychoanalytic model to understand the developmental implications of the pathological family system and to understand that what we see clinically at times is the patient's *adaptation to that system*, an adaptation that has pathological sequelae. To interpret these sequelae from the point of view of the individual's psychology apart from that system will constitute a serious failure to understand the individual. Her internal world will contain the complexities and paradoxes of the pathological family system. Until these issues are confronted in therapy, the individual will remain hostage to the system no matter how much work is done from the perspective of individual development.

The dynamics of the pathological family system will inevitably capture the developing child, usually at that point at which she has emerged out of the total dependency of infancy and begins to take on the unique characteristics of the small child, characteristics that more or less determine what is projected onto the child and what role is assigned to her. In addition to developing these characteristics, the child develops language, enabling the verbal communication that also becomes a major vehicle for shaping the child into her role.

The Double-Bind on Achievement: Slipp

Slipp (1984) describes the complexities of the family system and its relationship to what will present clinically as the core relationship problem. An example of this is the situation in neurotic depression in which the child is made responsible, through projective identification, for the self-esteem of the parent. The child is pressured to succeed so that the parent can experience vicarious gratification that bolsters his lagging self-esteem. These parents can proudly show off the child's achievement as if it were their own. These parents borrow and take ownership of the success of the child, to puff themselves up and thus remedy their own sense of failure.

But, and it is a significant but, the very success of the child is then envied, and because of the envy, is not validated. No matter what the child achieves, it is never quite good enough. That which is envied is spoiled so as to render it no longer enviable, and the spoiler regains a sense of superiority from the position of the critic.

The lack of validation interferes with the child's ability to own his own success, and keeps him dependently tied to the parent in hopes of getting the validation. Because failure would result in rejection and success is not acknowledged as good enough, no matter what the child does, he cannot win. The child experiences a learned helplessness because of this double-bind and is deprived of a sense of mastery and satisfaction. This double-bind on achievement vis-à-vis the parent is internalized by the neurotic depressive. The child then treats himself as he was treated by the parent: failure results in severe loss of self-esteem, and success is never good enough.

Working with the Double-Bind on Achievement in Therapy

When we work with an individual whom we see to be doubly conflicted in the realm of achievement and success as described by Slipp, we need to ask what the core relationship problem is that is embedded in what seems to be a purely internal situation. This frees the treatment from the impasse of the internalized double-bind and leads to exploration of the relational context in which the dilemma arose and of how it is manifest in present day situations, including the transference.

The double-bind was first articulated by Bateson, Jackson, Haley, and Weakland (1956). The child is trapped by hopelessly conflicting injunctions from the mother. And there is a third ingredient in a double-bind—the implicit injunction that the contradiction is not to be noticed or commented upon. The content of the contradictory messages will vary from situation to situation, but the net effect is the same. For example, the messages may tell the child she must both succeed and fail, she must be both dependent and independent, or she must be both sexual and asexual.

If we take this example of having to succeed and fail and consider the effect on the child's sense of self *in relation to* the significant other, we find contradictory self-states that parallel the contradictory injunctions. There are the overvalued self that carries the pride of the parent and the devalued self that carries the parent's shame. Generally, these irrational role assignments do not come into play (Framo, 1970) until the child has reached the age where language begins to play a role and the evolving uniqueness of the child is more salient. Talents, constitutional factors, and temperament will lend themselves to service parental fantasies, both fears and wishes. For example, if a mother who has all boys selects one of them to take the role of the wished-for daughter, she is not likely to choose the robust, action-oriented son but the quieter one who is more content to read or color with her. Conversely, a father who has all daughters may select one of them to be the wished-for son, and here it will be the larger, more action-oriented girl who becomes his companion when he goes hunting or fishing. On those expeditions she is "one of the guys." She perceives she is treated differently from her sisters and may take pleasure in the implication of her specialness to her father. Paradoxically, it is as his quasi-son that she triumphs in her rivalry as a female over the other females. This child may become confused with respect to gender, and on the one hand she may be thrown into greater turmoil at puberty when her femaleness cannot be denied. On the other hand, she may actually be relieved at the biological support of her sense of self as a girl, yet be in conflict in her relationships with men, not sure which they want her to be, the feminine self she feels to be her nature or the masculine self that her father projected onto her.

The true self (Winnicott, [1960] 1965a) of the child creates a third self-state that may or may not be conscious. As an adult the individual who has been double-bound as described by Slipp may exhibit a paralysis, unable to move either toward success or toward failure. Each evokes severe anxiety, which is relational insofar as it pertains to the link with the parent in question. Self-sabotage may be evident when there is a threat of success. Compensatory pride-restoring fantasies or behaviors may take over when there is a threat of failure. The individual's life has a Ping-Pong quality, as she goes back and forth from one side of the dilemma to the other. This situation can be especially puzzling when the individual is clearly capable of a very high level of achievement.

Inevitably, the dilemma has its effect on the treatment process. The goal of the treatment and the action of the therapist are, from the patient's point of view, not neutral at all, especially when the therapist actively supports and encourages the moves toward success. A negative therapeutic reaction (Chapter Fifteen) can be expected when the success of the therapy threatens the bond with the parent who needs the patient to fail. Yet, if the therapist attends too much to failure, the patient will feel shamed. The dilemma has to be interpreted with a fleshing out of the family system, which is more than likely still in effect. It is not unusual to find a multigenerational component: the mother played a similar role with the grandmother and now is in the other seat, so to speak, replaying the scenario with her daughter with roles reversed. Paying attention to such multigenerational dynamics is necessary for the systems perspective that will enable the patient to separate who she is from the roles and identities that have been assigned her and the identities that she has chosen for herself in the family of origin.

Projective Identification in the Family System

The extensive use of the mechanism of *projective identification* can be seen in the pathological family dynamic. For example, the mother may project her grandiose self into her child as well as her shameful and devalued self. The child's introjection of these projections and identification with them creates the different self-states associated with each of the several identities. Meanwhile, the true self of the child becomes split off and even lost in the process. These self-states will be reenacted with others later in life, with the individual chronically and intensely anxious about being shamed or being able to restore pride vis-à-vis the other. Relationships so structured do not allow for authentic or genuine connection. The individual, at heart, feels isolated and alone. Because of the prominence of shame-pride issues, the person may be misdiagnosed as having a narcissistic personality disorder. The apparent pathology of self-esteem is the result of the child's identification with the mother's projections.

A parent may also project into the child a disowned hated self, such as his needy self. He then criticizes and attacks the child for what he needs her to be for his own sense of well-being. In other situations what is projected is the parent's own hated or feared persecutory object representation. The child is then viewed as the persecutor and ragefully attacked, being blamed for all of the parent's distress.

The structure and relational setup of the isolated true self will depend on the point at which the original derailment took place. The same mother might be a superb mother of infancy but fail with an individuating child. It is important not to lose sight of the relationship piece of the puzzle. In the family system setup these several states may not be dissociated as in those cases described in Chapter Eight. This makes the analytic exploration of them less stormy although it does not follow that the resolution will be easy. The patient will have unconscious wishes and fears with respect to the parent and in the transference as well that will have to be uncovered and analyzed in the course of the therapy.

Slipp also describes the role of family savior that may be assigned to a particular child. Either it is her job to keep the family together or her job to keep her mother together so the mother can function as the others in the family need her to. The child in question is left with two contradictory views of the self as well. She is told that she is omnipotent, that she has the power to save her mother. But she also becomes aware that she has no power to do this at all, that she is doomed to failure no matter how hard she tries. So she goes back and forth between states of omnipotence and impotence, believing both and failing to develop a realistic sense of what she can and cannot do within the relationship as well as in the world at large. If she makes any move toward independence, toward a refusal to take her assigned responsibility, she may be told that she is killing her mother or making her mentally ill. We may find the entire family, including extended family members, converging upon her and pressuring her with anxiety and guilt to return to the symbiotic arrangement with her mother. Of course, this lets them off the hook. The analytic work will deal with this patient's confusions about herself, and we are likely to find the underlying depression of the abandoned and unprotected true self emerging as we go along.

It is possible for the therapist to lay out the several selves and the mother with whom each self is connected. For example: "Your highly achieving self is connected with the mother who boasts about you. Your despised failure self is connected with the mother who is ashamed of you. The confusion about who you really are is connected to the mother who fails to see you and to confirm your intrinsic worth and identity, who abandons you when you do not play your assigned role. And your grieving, frightened self is connected to the lost mother of infancy who loved you until you developed a mind and will of your own—a self separate and apart from her."

This is not unlike the interpretive formulation, the cognitive aspect of working with dissociated self-states as described in Chapter Eight. Obviously, the work must have led up to the point where this formulation can be made. It cannot come ex cathedra from a therapist who is unable to wait and let the process unfold. Instead, there comes a time of readiness when the formulation has to be made and set forth as core relationship conflicts that engineer the patient's way of being in the world. In the kind of situation just described, there are two levels of core conflict: one at the original point of derailment and another that comes out of the necessity of adapting to parental pathology in subsequent years. The therapist works toward the goal of conflict resolution with respect to the object and toward integration with respect to the self.

It is nearly impossible for the child to individuate out of the pathological family system without paying the price of loss of family, loss of the object, or loss of the object's love. There is no internal good object to support the individuating self. In more severe cases the sense of self is so impoverished that separation anxiety keeps the individual within the system for survival even though, paradoxically, the cost of that survival is the loss of the true self. The conditions of survival are actually antithetical to survival.

Binding

Stierlin (1974) describes the ways adolescent individuation is blocked when "parents and children operate under the unspoken assumption that essential satisfactions and securities can be obtained only within the family. . . . [P]arents . . . see only one avenue open to them: to tie their children ever more closely to themselves" (p. 36). He describes three forms of binding. In *id binding*, exploitation of dependency needs is enabled by emphasis on regressive gratification. The adolescent is infantilized. *Ego binding* results as a consequence of the child's being made to feel doubtful and insecure about his own resources. The parent interferes with the child's differentiated self-awareness and self-determination through mystification and violation of cognitive integrity—undercutting the child's confidence in his ability to think. *Superego binding* exploits loyalty, and guilt over wishes to break away is instilled ("How can you do that to me?" "Don't you know you're killing your mother?"). Children are turned into lifelong self-sacrificing victim-adjuncts.

The relationship conflicts we are likely to observe clinically will have to do with the wish to have relationships or loves outside the family and with the anxieties associated with each of the modes of binding. The individual will be unwilling to give up the gratification of the infantile emotional goodies, or will be too frightened at the prospect of negotiating the world on his own, or will be too guilty at even the wish to separate. As a patient the individual is likely to experience the therapist as pushing him toward any one of these dangers. In such an instance we may come up against the negative therapeutic reaction, in which therapeutic success seems to make the person worse (see Chapter Fifteen).

In the case of the active family system pressures, we are not dealing with past developmental conflicts and their residua; the conflicts are hot and heavy in the present, and the cast of characters is still strongly acting upon the individual to render him unable to break away. *We cannot analyze the real.* If a parent is paying for the treatment, it is not likely to survive. If we can engage the seeds of autonomy striving in the alliance and if the individual can get a job and pay for his own treatment, the prognosis is better. At that point the conflicts can be brought into the treatment relationship where the core relationship problems can be more successfully explored.

Faced with the kinds of relationship difficulties that exist in the context of pathological family dynamics, we need to think about two linked core relationship problems. The first entails the family requirements for interpersonal connection. We will see how this way of being relationally is acted out with others in general and with us in the transference. If the individual is required to be stupid for his mother to feel intellectually superior, he will be stupid with us. We are likely to feel immensely frustrated as the process becomes mired in this dynamic.

The second core relationship problem involves the split-off true self and the fear of relating from that self-state. Our task is to engage with this facet of the individual's personality and to allow it to come into relationship with us. This may be a stormy process, but it is where the work must be done.

Therapists other than those who identify themselves as behavioral-cognitive in their theoretical orientation, often tend to dismiss or devalue the cognitive aspects of the person's mind. These aspects become suspect as manifestations of defensiveness. Instead, emotions are deemed the gold of treatment. But emotion divorced from thought, as well as thought divorced from emotion, is only half the picture. The child not only experiences and feels; he or she also explains each experience to himself or herself and then comes to *believe* those explanations. The next chapter focuses on the cognitive side of the core relationship problem—the individual's belief system about what people and relationships are like.

Chapter Five

Belief Systems and the Analytic Work

Early on, Freud ([1894] 1953a) noted the problems that ensue when affect and cognition are defensively split off from each other. In both obsessional and hysterical neurosis, there is such a split between cognition—what Freud called the content of an idea— and affect. He wrote at that time that in hysteria the person gets rid of affect by conversion and has no consciousness of the content of the idea. In the obsessional neurosis, although affect is retained, it is split off from the content of the idea and a substitute idea is found with which to link it (p. 211).

A factor that plays a role in the traumatizing effect of intense affect on the baby or toddler is the absence of a cognitive framework within which affect may be structured. Yet when we talk about the importance of cognition in the clinical work, the assumption may be made that we are referring to cognitive-behavioral therapy or that we are using intellectualizing defenses. Humans are meaning-making creatures, and the present-day focus on the role of the signifier and what it signifies (Horner, 1995) refocuses us on the central place of the cognitive processes. Whereas the individual signifier (word) contains a wealth of meaning, the belief system carries even further weight.

The author gratefully acknowledges permission to reprint this chapter, with slight adaptations, which was originally published in the *American Journal of Psychoanalysis*, 1997, 57, 75–78. Copyright © 1997 by the Association for the Advancement of Psychoanalysis.

Belief systems are set up in early childhood and come out of a combination of the experiences of the child within the environment and the limited thinking and reasoning of which the child is capable as she tries to make sense of her universe. These belief systems lead to fears and expectations and subsequent adaptations to these fears and adaptations. That is, as much as feelings lead to thoughts and beliefs, thoughts and beliefs also generate feelings. The mind is convoluted, nonlinear, and often paradoxical. The more mystified the child is about what the world is like, the more she will depend upon her belief systems and the more she will seek certainty and predictability by organizing around them. This attempt will lead to characterological rigidity as the child attempts to control uncertainty and unpredictability. Pop psychology, such as the current bestseller that tells us that men are from Mars and women are from Venus, has some of its appeal insofar as it provides ready-made belief systems. The belief system becomes the basic premise upon which logic rests, but of course if any syllogism has a false basic premise, its conclusion will also be false. Also, any generalization about a class of individuals will surely lead to false assumptions about many specific individuals. These assumptions will activate expectations, feelings, fears and wishes, or defenses that will make an authentic relationship impossible. This is what happens in the case of prejudice (prejudgment). Thus there is a downside to seeking certainty and predictability.

We all have unconscious belief systems, and by and large they address a core of beliefs that orients us to the world and our way of being in the world. *For each self and object relationship structure, along with characteristic linking affect, there will also be characteristic linking thought and belief. Belief systems arise within an interpersonal matrix and thus will be directly or indirectly relational in their assumptions.* In our therapeutic work we will find

- Beliefs about the self
    What am I like?
- Beliefs about others

What are other people like?

What are girls (women) like?

What are boys (men) like?

What are authority figures like?

- Beliefs about what I have to do (be like) to connect to the other?
- Beliefs about what I have to do (be like) to be safe?
- Beliefs about what I have to do (be like) to be secure in a relationship?
- Beliefs about what I have to do (be like) to be able to feel good about myself?
- Beliefs about what I have to do (be like) to have my wishes come true?
- Beliefs about what I have to do (be like) to prevent my fears from coming true?

The patient's belief system can be a heavy hand upon the therapeutic process, contributing to transference resistance—that way of relating to the therapist aimed at bringing about a wished-for interaction or preventing a feared interaction.

Bromberg's observation (1996a) that we do not treat patients "to cure them of something that was done to them in the past; rather, we are trying to cure them of what they still do to themselves and to others in order to *cope* with what was done to them in the past" (p. 70) leads us to a more dynamic perspective than a unidimensional, blaming historical perspective. The individual's adaptations or intrapsychic and interpersonal strategies may be useful insofar as they bring about the desired end results, although the more extensive these adaptations are, the higher the price a person pays for them. That is, there is a cost-benefit ratio. The higher the cost to a person's mental well-being, to the ability to relate satisfactorily with others, and to the ability to pursue and achieve goals and interests, the more the person has to address the underlying issues (the belief systems and how they came about) in order to change his or her life. Because everyone has these issues to contend with to a greater or lesser degree, the question is where along this cost-benefit continuum each person's own issues lie.

Here are a few illustrative examples (far from a complete list) of beliefs that can determine a person's way of being in the world.

- If I don't do what the other wants, or agree with her or him, I will be attacked or abandoned.

- If I have what I want, someone else will envy me and will attack me, abandon me, or take it away from me.

- If I try to compete I will be killed.

- If I show I need the other person, I will be in her or his power. I can control the other person by showing I don't need her or him.

- My mother had my sister and brother after me because I just wasn't enough.

- There must be something terribly wrong with me if my own mother couldn't love me.

- My mother didn't love me because I didn't do it right. (The postulation of a nonexistent "it" is born of mystification.)

Sometimes a core belief like one of these is hidden for some time before it slips into the patient's associations. The alert therapist will not miss the significance of this quietly expressed assumption and will identify it before it disappears from awareness again. Such beliefs will be an inherent factor in the core relationship problem. They should alert the therapist to the importance of putting them into a relationship perspective.

It is not difficult to imagine what the consequences of these beliefs may be for an individual's life. The therapy process reveals these belief systems: how they came about and how they are played out in the here-and-now as well as what the consequences are for playing them out. Although any analyst or therapist may note that there is nothing unfamiliar about this way of thinking, what is proposed here is a more active role on the part of the therapist in the articulation of these belief systems *as belief systems*, along with laying out their consequences for the individual. This is not an interpretation so much as a highlighting of that which the person already "knows," (that is, believes) in a way that allows him or her to work with the "knowledge" and reevaluate its validity. Placing the belief system squarely in the context of the core relationship problem makes it possible to do the work. We do not get into arguments about the relative validity of each belief per se.

One consulting therapist reported how after four years of a stormy course of therapy that seemed to be unproductive beyond supporting the patient and providing a holding environment, the setting forth of the patient's organizing belief system propelled the treatment to a new level. The patient's mother had taught her that it is not good to dwell on feelings or to express them, that she should just get over them. This injunction mystified and frightened the child she was, and she developed intense anxiety about the *something awful* that would happen if she let herself feel or let herself say what she felt. The fear was born of mystification and magical thinking. When the therapist articulated this belief as a belief that had governed the patient's way of being in the world, the patient herself, with great excitement, laid out the entire array of what had come about as its result. This specific delineation of the role of this belief in her psychology was the linchpin that brought together the pieces they had talked about for years into a coherent whole. A dream that was clearly a transference dream but had been denied as such could be explored after the articulation of the belief system that had motivated the resistance to understanding the dream. Anchoring the belief within the core relationship conflict vis-à-vis the patient's mother demystified the belief.

As I have mentioned, there is a tendency to elevate feelings above thinking in therapeutic circles. "How did you feel about that" is more likely to be the inquiry of choice than is, "How did you explain that to yourself?" But it can be important to understand how later events and experiences are assimilated into preexisting belief systems and are then interpreted as confirmation of them. Furthermore, individuals who are not psychologically sophisticated can more quickly grasp an approach based upon how they think and reason than a formulation tinged with theoretical assumptions. And even psychologically sophisticated patients are likely to be unaware of the degree to which unconscious or unarticulated belief systems affect their lives.

If we think of the person's beliefs as data useful for assessing the core relationship problem, we will not be put off by the individual who insists on the rationality of these beliefs.

This chapter has demonstrated cognitive manifestations of the core relationship conflict. In the next section, specific clinical issues are discussed from the relational perspective. This reveals how important these issues are as sources for understanding the person, which then makes them accessible to the work. The first one, the compromise formation, is especially valuable, providing a window into the complexities of the patient's mind and his or her core relationship problem.

Part Two

Some Common Clinical Problems and Issues

Chapter Six

Deciphering the
Compromise Formation

A Psychological Rosetta Stone

For hundreds of years the language of ancient Egypt had been a riddle to scholars. Then, in 1799, an officer of Napoleon's engineering corps unearthed what has come to be known as the Rosetta stone, near the mouth of the Nile River. On it was a decree by Ptolemy V, carved around 196 B.C. The inscription appeared in three languages; one was the then mysterious hieroglyphics of the ancient Egyptians, but one of the remaining two was ancient Greek. By translating the Greek and using it as guide, scholars were able to begin deciphering these ancient hieroglyphics.

Today the term *Rosetta stone* denotes that which holds the key to understanding in other puzzling situations as well. The meaning of a dream can often be deciphered by focusing on a single strange or bizarre element in the dream and finding what that strange image means to the dreamer. The seemingly out-of-place image can function as the Rosetta stone for the dream as a whole. A dream about a schoolmate of many years ago might bring the association, "She was the littlest kid in the class." The significance of the dream may be how the dreamer felt as the littlest one in his family growing up and how he felt that way again at a business meeting the day before.

In this chapter, I will view the compromise formation as the Rosetta stone that may reveal the nature of the core relationship conflict.

The Psyche-Soma Link

The classical understanding of the *compromise formation* is that it is a substitutive idea or act that represents all sides of a repressed conflict and creatively weaves together the separate elements of the conflict within an apparently cohesive whole. Its very usefulness in reducing felt dissonance is reinforcing of its power.

For example, in conceptualizing sexual perversion in Freudian terms, Stoller (1975) writes that the ego creates "a compromise formation that will (partially) gratify the instinctual wish while placating the superego or reality demands that the wish be gone" (p. 93).

If we consider the substitutive idea or act as encompassing the various elements of the core relationship conflict, rather than balancing id, ego, and superego forces, analysis of the compromise formation will elucidate that conflict and make it accessible to the analytic work. A particularly powerful compromise formation is that of the sexual fantasy.

As a powerful biological drive, sex has the ability to *capture* early unarticulated relationship conflicts, and sexual fantasies will then be a way for the individual to both symbolize and manage those conflicts. This eroticization of the psychological conflict embedded in the compromise formation creates a psyche-soma link that contributes further to the power of the compromise formation as a solution. Now that the individual views it as the key to sexual expression and gratification, he or she will be reluctant to bring it into question in treatment.

In her review of the work by Wrye and Welles (1994) on the *maternal erotic transference*, Person (1997) criticizes what she describes as their "collapsing sex and bonding into an undifferentiated 'erotic' transference" (p. 269). I agree with Person when she describes the "closely intertwined (but still separate) developmental lines for attunement and attachment, on the one hand, and for sexuality, on the other" (p. 270). Although communication may be transmitted through bodily feelings and sensations, it is the impairments in the processes of bonding and attachment that constitute the core relationship problem and that will be clinically relevant and interpretable.

McDougall (1974), exploring the intricate and inevitable connection of psyche and soma, describes how in the case of the conversion symptoms of hysteria, "the body lends itself and its functions to the mind to use as the mind wills" (p. 441). Perhaps one bright, imaginative six-year-old girl intuited this connection when she playfully said she had a factory in her head. Asked what she made there, she said, "Wild animals, so I will have the energy to exercise." In the case of the sexual fantasy, analysis of the compromise formation loosens the psyche-soma link and the erotic hold the substitutive act or idea has on the individual. The compromise formation that often takes the form of a particular sexual fantasy or act may contain the complexities of a particular family system dynamic in which the developing child was caught and that is related to the core relationship conflict or conflicts.

Masturbatory Fantasies

Exploration of masturbatory fantasies, although often uncomfortable for the therapist, can open up a rich and complex compromise formation. In some instances of analytic work with men who are committed to a heterosexual life, who feel and define themselves as heterosexual, we may find that they are nevertheless troubled by sexual fantasies of themselves with another man. I am describing a group of men who have no interest in finding a male life partner but whose obsessional fantasies are about men who are essentially faceless and interchangeable. A not uncommon theme is one in which the self is passive and even unwilling, but the powerful man of the fantasy overcomes the patient's resistances and dominates him sexually. Sometimes infliction of pain is also involved. The ability to bear the pain creates an illusion of strength that counteracts the weakness of submission. At one level this compromise formation functions as described by Stoller: desire is denied and placed in the other, and because one is forced to submit, there is no guilt. In some cases it is the wish for a particular other (father) rather than the demands of an impersonal id that must be denied, and it is the voice of the mother rather than that of the impersonal agency of the superego that creates guilt. That is, we take an interpersonal, relational approach to understanding the fantasy.

It is very important that the therapist not get sidetracked by some personal need to define this person as heterosexual or homosexual. Making this problem into an issue of sexual politics will further derail the treatment.

The Role of Family Schism

If we look further into a situation like that just described, we may find the family relationship system represented as well. For example, we may find that parental conflict and separation or divorce left the small boy with the mother. If he expressed a wish to see his father, his mother was angry at what she viewed as disloyalty and betrayal. To wish for his father had now become taboo and would lead to loss of his mother's love, so it had to be denied. The wish went underground, and the little boy hoped his father would want him enough to push pass his mother's interference. His father had to want him more than he did not want his father. But in many of these situations, the father opted out and left the boy with the possessive mother. The boy then felt he had to submit to her demands or face total abandonment and felt rejected and devalued by the father as well as a painful sense of loss of the father he had once loved. In addition the mother could not stand any traits in her son that reminded her of the father, and she let the boy know this. Then he not only had to not want his father, he had to not be like him—which was tantamount to not being masculine. The developmental identification with the father was blocked, an identification that would have established his sense of masculinity more firmly and that also would have mitigated the experience of loss. If we look at the fantasy again from an interpersonal perspective, it bypasses the mother's injunction against wanting the father so the son is not guilty of betrayal of his mother.

As an extension of this relationship problem, individuation from the mother in the broader sense also endangers the son's connection to her, and a feeling that he is trapped within her orbit ensues. Adult relationships with women are then viewed as potentially entrapping, and when this situation comes about in reality, the fantasy of sex with a man offers the illusion of escape. Furthermore, being desired by the man reassures him that he is wantable, although like the Don Juan of either gender, he has to prove this over and over and over. He can capture the desired father in essence by seducing him, by making the father substitute want him, although the seduction is denied and attributed to the other. In addition, as we often find in family situations like this, the sense of self as masculine is compromised. These patients will describe how physical union with a male partner acts as a temporary antidote to this felt deficit as the masculinity of the sex partner is borrowed and taken into the self during the sex act.

The deciphering of this sexual fantasy reveals how this man as a boy put together the separate elements of his family and relationship conflicts within the compromise formation (the sexual idea and/or the sexual act) and attained, for a brief time, a reduction of his inner dissonance and turmoil. The success of the solution along with the necessity of its being repeated over and over lends it the feeling of an addictive need.

As an incredibly complex psychological balancing act the compromise formation in this example contains the individual's core relationship conflicts associated with both parents—how to bypass the mother's taboo on individuation without losing her love and how to reach the unreachable father in order to repair the wounded self that is experienced as unwantable and unmasculine and to restore the father the individual once had and lost. The deciphering of the compromise formation makes all of these factors accessible to the analytic work. Sex is no longer the issue. The self in relation to others now takes center stage.

Compromise formations may be embedded in a variety of fantasies, symptoms, or behaviors. In relationship terms we may be able to discover the elements of wish, fear, and defense against what is feared. Relationship patterns may both connect and disconnect, revealing the wish and the defense. Hypothesizing a perhaps unconscious danger that requires the defense of disconnecting, exploration can be directed toward discovery of what it might be. Hostile dependency is an example of such a compromise. The hostility preserves the sense of separateness or autonomy that might be lost if the wish were acted upon in an undefended way. Another example is that of the woman who weighed three hundred pounds—in part to spite her mother who wanted her to be thin, in part to be sure everyone noticed her, and in part to hide her true, vulnerable self. As a dynamic this is very different from the dynamic of the eating disorder, although on presentation that might come to mind as a diagnosis. Eating disorders are discussed later in this book as obsessional disorders in which not only the importance of the other but even the existence of the other may be denied and the battle appears to be with the body and its desires, whereas in motivated obesity the conflicted relationship is very much in the foreground.

Such complex behaviors carry both the core relationship problem and the individual's solution (not *resolution*) to the problem.

Like the compromise formation, symptoms are also rich in what they both reveal and conceal. Unlocking the core relationship problem embedded in the symptom is critical for the work. In the light of current advances in technology, especially in the field of neurology, the psychological implications of symptoms may be overlooked in the enthusiasm about new biological finds. The next chapter addresses this conflict of approaches with respect to the obsessive-compulsive disorder.

Chapter Seven

OCD

The Medicalization of Psychopathology and the Importance of Preserving a Psychology of the Mind

With the increasing emphasis on neurology and a pharmacological approach to treatment, the existence of obsessive-compulsive behaviors is now said to signify a biologically caused disorder, and treatment is recommended accordingly—that is through a pharmacological approach. The goal of preserving the concept of a psychology of the mind as well, reminds us to examine obsessive-compulsive symptoms from that perspective.

The Obsessive Personality

In 1968, writing about the *obsessive personality*, Leon Salzman departed from Freud's view of the symptom as a device for dealing with unacceptable hostile or sexual impulses and instead presented his own view of "the obsessional maneuver as an adaptive technique to protect the person from the exposure of any thought or feeling that will endanger his physical or psychological existence" (p. 14). He noted that this formulation does not require the postulate of an instinct or libido theory. He also observed that as a *style*, obsessional patterns range all the way from normal to psychotic. With respect to psychopathology, he refers to the obsessive *defense* and how it provides a feeling of security in a world in which uncertainty is inevitable.

Recent advances in technology have opened up the workings of the brain to neurological researchers. Unfortunately, these discoveries have been used in the denial of difficult intrapsychic and interpersonal conflicts. One does not see an individual with conflict, anxiety, and defense; one sees a sick patient with a disease that requires medical (pharmacological) intervention.

The Causal Link

At a panel presentation at the California Institute of Technology (*Images of Mental Illness*, 1996), slides were shown illustrating the coincidence of certain brain changes and what was called OCD (obsessive-compulsive disorder). The causal link was explicitly articulated, that brain changes do allegedly *cause* the psychological disorder. The moderator of the distinguished panel of scientists subsequently reported on the evening television news that compulsive gambling had now been proven to be caused by problems in the brain.

But anyone with any sophistication in statistical analysis will know that the cause-effect link—if there is indeed one—could just as well go in the other direction: that is, the obsessional disorder and its affective components may cause changes in the brain. We are all familiar with the way in which mental activity of the mind affects the brain as seen in the creation of visual images in dreams even though the eyes are closed. The mind bypasses the sensory receptors. There is even a third alternative: that there is no causal link either way but that both factors covary through a connection with a third factor. The statistical device known as analysis of variance, or analysis of covariance, attempts to answer just such scientific questions.

When science sets out to prove a preformed conclusion, science itself must be called into question. The desire for certainty alluded to by Salzman (1968) plays a part when people seize upon a neurological explanation for a sometimes difficult to treat psychological problem. Younger psychotherapists are often eager to attach to the definitive and easier answer. When I hear someone use the term OCD in discussing a clinical problem, I generally find the person has accepted the medical diagnosis, the neurological explanation, and the pharmacological approach to treatment, often eschewing the psychological underpinnings of the disorder. From this person's perspective, the disorder is a *disease* and not an indication of conflict, anxiety, and defense. Yet obsession is treatable from the perspective that it is a *psychological* problem with a *psychological* solution. The relational, interpersonal understanding and clinical work that I am describing in this book prevents the therapist from becoming embroiled in the content of the obsession and allows an analytic approach.

A television news show in May of 1997 featured a story about children with severe obsessive-compulsive disorders. The brain changes were demonstrated, the implication being that this kind of disorder is a biological disease. The children were being treated with drugs and were in group therapy, coming together as kids who all had this same disease. It was reassuring to each child to feel he or she was not the only one with the disorder. Now there was a name for his or her distress—OCD. A self-image as someone with a disease would be the outcome, and attention to family dynamic factors would be absent. Secondary gain would likely be the result, as the family could now focus on the child's illness and its treatment. The identified patient had now been assigned his or her role within the family system. The core relationship problem would go even further underground.

Yet similar symptoms in other children have been noted to be the outcome of anxieties over conflict with the parent or parents. The child who is frantic at not being able to choose what to wear, for example, may well now be dealing with the derivative of her fear of doing the wrong thing and making her father angry at her. This would be especially true if she could not understand what it was that would set him off, if his mood or state of tiredness led to an angry loss of patience for ordinary everyday child behavior. It would be true with the alcoholic father, whose outbursts were unpredictable and terrifying. Not understanding what she had done wrong, the child would feel she had better be sure she did not do *anything* wrong, make any wrong choices. In how many of the families of these children was parental abuse of alcohol kept secret from the therapist?

In another manifestation of psychological conflict in the form of obsessional behavior, the fear of the loss of impulse control related to repressed anger may come out in the child's fears that he or she may have caused a fire by not turning the light switch off completely, leading to checking and rechecking the switch. To treat such children as having a medical disease and to fail to treat underlying relational anxieties is, in my view, negligent at best.

Relationship Factors in OCD

In our clinical work we need to begin with an interpretation of the *function* of the obsession. It is a *defense mechanism* and has been understood as such since Freud, although our understanding of what is being defended against has changed over time. Leaving behind the archaic assumptions of instinct theory and drawing from all we have learned about the development of the self within the context of human relationship, we can understand the defense as protecting the individual from the anxieties or guilt inherent in the problem relationship setup, that is, the core relationship conflict.

The obsession, like a magnet, draws all attention, cognitive and emotional, away from where the conflict lies, focusing it elsewhere and providing a magical solution to the unresolved conflict or conflicts. Of course this does not fix the problem because the solution is an illusion, a displacement, and offers only temporary respite from the distresses associated with the core conflict—thus the need to return to the solution again and again and again and the formation of an obsession.

Along with our interpretation of the defensive function of the obsession, we make a formulation of the *interpersonal* features of this core conflict that are relevant to the specifics of the individual's developmental history and internal object relations.

We might have a patient who is obsessed with the seeming hyperacuity of her olfactory senses and the fear that what she smells will be toxic to her, eventually to discover in our exploration her underlying fear of her father when she could smell alcohol on his breath. The psychological toxicity of the milieu in which she grew up could be denied or repressed, and the hard work of confronting its psychological aftermath could be avoided. As a child she may have developed a stance of vigilance in order to protect herself from her father's frightening behavior; if she smelled alcohol, she could either be very quiet or could hide. This vigilance with respect to smell might then have led to a heightened acuity of that sensory apparatus, much as a blind person develops a heightened sensitivity to sound. Endangered from within by her internalized persecutory objects against which she would have no defense, she could derive a false sense of security from trying to protect herself from smells in the environment.

In a similar vein, obsessional hypochondriacal fears that one's body will turn against one by developing cancer or some other life-threatening illness may be seen in some cases as a defense against the recognition and acknowledgment of the mother's hatred or hostility. The development of pain in a woman's breast whenever something good happened could be a somatic response to her mother's envious hatred and her fear of an attack by her mother, recalling McDougall's statement (1974) that "the body lends itself and its functions to the mind to use as the mind wills" (p. 441). In the course of therapy the emergence of awareness of the hatred by and toward the mother may be accompanied by stormy hypochondriacal obsession and symptoms.

Eating disorders are essentially obsessions, once again involving the body. Bulimia can be understood in terms of interpersonal conflict as a double approach-avoidance conflict involving both parents (discussed further later in this chapter). On one hand we find a wish-fear conflict involving the mother, and on the other a wish-fear conflict involving the father. The bulimia is also a compromise formation, allowing for both expression of desire for the object and defensive rejection of the object. Uncovering the separate and distinct wish-fear component relevant to *each* parent is critical.

Smoking often takes on an obsessional quality, perhaps being labeled an addiction. The fear of cancer does not deter, for in fact that fear is a significant piece of the complex dynamic. Whatever the physiologically addictive qualities of nicotine may be, it is the psychological dynamic that has a hold on the individual. I have found in many cases that the person in question long ago submitted to the relationship rule that he has no right to have a wish or desire of his own and that if he does express one, the narcissistic mother will be enraged. His role is to fit himself into her psychological drama and scenario, to tend to her wishes and desires. With all other avenues of desire blocked, now by the internalized forbidding mother, desire discovers an outlet, the cigarette. He can have what he wants when he wants it. There is an illusion of control.

However, a compromise formation may develop (see Chapter Six) that contains both the wish and the punishment for gratifying the wish (cancer). The cancer that will attack the body and destroy him is a signifier for the attacking mother. Sometimes another obsession is formed around the punishment factor, and the fear of cancer becomes a hypochondriacal preoccupation. The union of the obsessional dynamic with that of the compromise formation creates a powerful motivational system that seems to have a life of its own, unless and until there is an uncovering of the core relationship conflict vis-à-vis the narcissistic mother contained in both.

The Double Approach-Avoidance Conflict

Other obsessional behaviors may take the form of an inability to choose between alternatives. Here the concept of the double approach-avoidance conflict is especially useful, as we see in the instance of bulimia.

An *approach-avoidance conflict* exists when a person is simultaneously attracted to and repelled by a single goal object (Munn, Fernald, and Fernald, 1972). As the person moves closer to the goal on the basis of the attraction or desirability of the object, the strength of the repelling force gets stronger, reaching a point at which an avoidant turning away from the goal or object is mobilized. Then, as the individual gets farther and farther from what is desired, anxiety is reduced and the attraction, wish, or desire asserts itself once again, and again the direction of movement is reversed. Obviously, this situation may pertain to relationship conflict, manifested by both a wish for and fear of the object or of the relationship setup as it has been historically established.

A *double approach-avoidance conflict* exists when the individual has both positive and negative attitudes toward *two* goals that have come to be experienced or perceived as mutually exclusive, with the same opposing forces operating in relation to both goals or objects. This relationship dilemma may come into being at various levels of psychological development.

During differentiation at the earliest stage, inherent strivings of the self may be accompanied by the threat of object loss and a consequent loss of cohesion of the self, and movement back toward the object may restore the sense of cohesion at the cost of the loss of identity of a separate self.

An unsuccessful resolution of the rapprochement phase of the separation-individuation process leaves the individual both drawn to and repelled by movement closer to the object and by movement away from the object. The dependent wish is countered by a fear of engulfment or loss of autonomy. The wish for autonomy is countered by fear of loss of the object or of the object's love, which engenders intense separation anxiety or depression.

The obsessive stasis of the oedipal situation is one in which the wish for the mother is countered by the fear of loss of the father and the loss of his love and developmental support or by fear of his anger and punishment. The wish for the mother may also be countered by its regressive implications. Furthermore, the wish for the father may also be countered by the fear of either the loss of the mother or the loss of her love. Essentially, to have mother is to lose father, and to have father is to lose mother. Sexual anxieties may also activate the avoidance response.

The confluence of the pre-oedipal and oedipal levels intensifies the double approach-avoidance situation. The child may fear that steps toward individuation will signify emotional abandonment to her mother, and if she turns to her father, her mother will view her as a treacherous rival as well.

Passage through these critical phases is inherently conflictual for the small child, and when the primary caretakers do not lend their encouragement and support because of their own relationship problems, the emergence of obsessional stalemates is all the more likely.

Despite differences in individuals' underlying character structures, the clinical pictures may look the same—the inability to make decisions and obsessive rumination on the possibility of making the "wrong" decision. From the point of view of the double approach-avoidance conflict, *any* decision has an inherent wrongness to it. A stage-appropriate interpretation of the underlying developmental and relationship dilemma is necessary to a resolution of the impasse and a subsiding of the obsessional symptomatology.

Once they place an emphasis on the *interpersonal* nature of the core conflict that is embodied within the obsession, both patient and therapist will be freed from the helplessness and frustration of persevering dead-end thinking and behaviors, allowing the analytic work to proceed. The treatment itself will still carry all the difficulties of dealing with disturbed relationship patterns both in terms of transference and countertransference, but at least the patient and the therapist can feel movement rather than the impotence of being caught in the obsession itself.

Often the approach to understanding a symptom and to working with it depends on the therapist's theoretical assumptions. If we understand obsessive-compulsive disorders from the perspective of the core relationship problem, our work will take us in that direction. The same principle is true with respect to dissociated self-states and theoretical disagreement as to the nature of the self. The next chapter deals with dissociated self-states from the perspective of a complex core relationship setup.

Chapter Eight

Working with
Dissociated Self-States

Before we can talk about our clinical approach to working with dissociated self-states, it is important that we first consider some of the theoretical issues.

The Theoretical Dialogue

There is a clamor of controversy in the current literature around the concept of an integrated self. A recent (1996) issue of the journal *Contemporary Psychoanalysis* was dedicated to the question. A symposium panel was invited to "to consider and investigate the evolving contemporary model of a postmodern self as decentered and disunified: in short, a normative multiple self." Panel members were asked "to reflect on whether 'the multiplicity of self' was a current fad, a misdirection, or an important paradigm shift" (Pizer, 1996, p. 499).

When those who say, "No, there is no such thing as an integrated self," appear to equate "integration" with "homogenization," their statement is invalidated at the outset. We all know that we experience ourselves differently depending on the situation. How I experience myself as I write this chapter is very different from the way I experience myself when I am cooking a holiday meal for my family or when I am tending my roses. Each of these situations is what Bromberg (1994) focuses on as a *self-state*. Yet, as I write this, I can, in my mind, go from one self-state to another quite comfortably, without losing my sense that "this is me."

Sutherland ([1989] 1994) writes how Fairbairn spoke of the *central ego*, defining it as the "residue of the undivided ego," the original ego. Fairbairn called it the *I*, seeing it as "comprised of conscious, preconscious, and unconscious elements. He emphasized its conscious nature" (p. 21). Moreover, "Fairbairn accepted that 'self' is a more appropriate term in most of his considerations, since it refers to the whole from which sub-selves are split off." Sutherland adds that "with a sub-self becoming dominant, it is difficult to specify where the 'autonomy' of the self is then located. Even under strong compulsions, there is usually an awareness of the situation of being 'possessed,' as though the observing self remains intact though powerless to exert enough control over it" (p. 26).

In the *Contemporary Psychoanalysis* symposium, Frank Lachmann (1996) was the lone voice speaking for the concept of an integrated self, a concept and position that if accepted will ultimately influence the therapist's work. He writes (and I agree with him): "One or another of a person's organizing themes may be in the foreground while others provide a background. Integration is not a melting pot that dissolves distinctions, but a mosaic that holds disparate facets of the self together. Integration does not entail pressure to yield up complexity, as critics of the singular self claim, but a tolerance for diversity. In striving for integration, characteristic and pervasive themes, divergent and conflicting states, wishes, affects, and ideas are encompassed. In fact this very fluidity is tolerable and sustainable when a sense of self-unity provides the background" (p. 597).

This condition cannot be better explicated than through the words of the patient who said: "When I first went into therapy I felt I'd been different people depending on who I was around. There was no connector between different phases of my life. Now there is a stronger sense of a 'me' there that ties them all together."

With respect to the work itself, Lachmann goes on to say that in his clinical work he presumes *a striving for an integrated self*. And he also points out that "holding an assumption of a striving for self-integration does not preclude my understanding of a variety of self-states, self-perceptions, and self-deceptions, including those that have been disavowed, embroiled in conflict, or suffused with shame" (p. 602). He enters the analytic dialogue with the assumption that the individual's self-states may be "facets of a complex self that is dominated by rigidly organized themes."

Bromberg (1996b), speaking for the concept of multiplicity of selves, pays attention to the existence of various self-states but applies the term *dissociation* to normal everyday shifts (such as those I just described with respect to myself) as well as to the more pathological and rigidly separated states found in clinical practice. I believe that making a distinction between the normal everyday shifts and pathological dissociation is far more useful.

In addition the fact that shifting self-states can be observed in infants does not preclude Lachmann's idea of a striving for integration or the idea that this striving would be present from the start. I personally observed such shifting states in a six-week-old infant I was holding in order to comfort him. He suddenly heard the loud ticking of a nearby clock and became quiet, riveting his attention on the clock. He then went back to screaming. He clearly shifted from attending on one hand to his internal discomfort and on the other hand to a sound in the external environment that caught his interest. The ability to shift attention from inner to outer later in life does not require or imply multiple selves.

Lachmann's view of the individual striving for an integrated self certainly applies to the human infant and is consistent with my own view that this striving is present from the start. Just as nature abhors a vacuum, the mind abhors disorganization. Although the infant is born with the equipment to perceive and organize what goes on around him, he has the monumental task of bringing what goes on within himself and in the external environment and what goes on between him and the other into some kind of organization. This process of organization underlies the build-up of the character structure, the structuring of the ego, and the establishment of the self and the other as internal structures. This striving to organize and the ability to do so is intrinsic to the organism. These mental activities take place as a consequence of the synthesizing function of the central nervous system, which is the physiological substrate of what ego psychologists call the *synthetic function* of the ego. However, this inborn and autonomous biological function can be interfered with by an inherent inadequacy of the organism (some defect in the brain itself) or by failure of the environment, or by a combination of the two.

Application in Practice

Bromberg (1996b) alerts us to the importance of attending to subtle and not so subtle shifting states within the clinical hour as well as trying to understand each of these states from an analytic perspective. I have observed at times a shift in states that suggests a dynamic relationship between them. An example of this is the emergence of a rageful, ruthless self that suddenly changes to a passive, complaining victim self. We might find that what is intolerable to the individual in the first is the fear of her destructiveness and guilt at its effect on the other person. The passivity of the victim posture protects self and other from out-of-control aggression and counteracts the guilt with the attitude of righteous indignation and moral superiority usually found in the victim posture.

Dissociated self-states will become manifest sooner or later in the clinical situation, and if the therapist is not prepared for these shifts, he can be thrown quite off balance, perhaps then using his own unique mechanisms for regaining a sense of equilibrium. The patient is likely to perceive these mechanisms negatively, perhaps as the therapist's abandonment of the patient or as the therapist's attempt to justify a hurt the patient has felt because of feeling misunderstood. Over time as the therapist becomes better acquainted with the various dissociated self-states of the patient, these disruptions are less likely to take place.

From the patient's point of view the existence of these dissociated self-states is particularly disruptive and maladaptive. *When any one self-state is present, the experience takes on a totality; it is all that is available to consciousness and is all that feels real.* Emotional and cognitive strengths and resources that are characteristic of a relatively positive state will be unavailable when the person is in a state of despair or catastrophic emergency.

If a therapist agrees that it is important that divergent self-states be worked with in a way to overcome the dissociative barriers and to help the individual toward her integration in the manner so well described by Lachmann, then that therapist's interventions will be aimed at doing so. As with any intervention the timing and manner will depend upon clinical sensitivity as well as on an intellectual understanding of what is to be dealt with.

Dissociated Self-States from a Relationship Perspective

Returning to the idea of the core relationship conflict, we can best understand the self-states from a relationship, or interpersonal, perspective. That is, *each separate self has its own connection with an aspect of the primary object and bears its own imprint of affect and thought.* Recall from the earlier chapters the perspective of object relations theory and the nature of internalized object relations, made up of both self and object representations with characteristic linking affect and cognition. Our understanding of dissociated self-states calls upon this same formulation, although of course dealing with far greater complexity.

When the patient, as a result of the work, gradually becomes aware and conscious of the coexistence of the several dissociated states, aware that they do indeed coexist and that they may even be in some dynamic relation to one another, the next step toward integration can be taken: that is, the direct attempt to link each state with a corresponding experience of the other in the formative years. A mother who herself manifests dissociated self-states leaves the young child little option but to *adapt to* each of the different mothers presented to her, perhaps leading to what Winnicott ([1962] 1965b) called a false self. In addition the child will inevitably *react to* the situation, perhaps with rage or despair.

The split-off buried baby of fantasy and dreams in such patients, as described by Guntrip (1971), can also be viewed as a dissociated self-state, often one that is repressed and out of awareness. Defensive and compensatory attempts may themselves lead to their own self-states. The child then has to cope with dissonant experiences of self as well. This, then, is the developmental origin of the dissociations that are brought into the clinical situation later on.

In addition to maternal psychopathology, traumatic dislocations such as the early death of parents and subsequent placement in foster homes, repeated hospitalizations, or other situations that lead to disruption of what Winnicott ([1962] 1965b) refers to as the sense of *going-on-being* may also lead to the same kind of dissociations.

In bringing together, with the patient, an integrative overview of his or her various states and all that is associated with them, I have found it useful to actually draw a diagram of the several states, each with the associated facet of the mother or primary caretaker(s). For example, I will draw circles labeled according to the individual's disparate experiences of the mother—for example, tender, hurtful, powerful, weak and in need of caretaking, adoring, contemptuous, or sexual. Then I will draw a connecting link to a symbol of each self-state that was experienced vis-à-vis each of these mothers. I find that this visual input to the cognitive work enhances the patient's deeper grasp of the formulation. I have also found that this approach can lead in fairly short order to a significant decrease in the dissociative phenomena and the ability then to deal with memory, feeling, conflict, and defense in a far less turbulent clinical ambience.

In this era of children's often changing caretakers, sitters, nannies, and day-care personnel, only time will tell if the clinician of twenty to thirty years from now will be dealing with the phenomena of dissociation to a far greater degree. In those headline cases in which judges wrest adoptive children from the only parents they have ever known to return them to their biological parent or parents, it would be most interesting to follow these children over the long range, despite the reports of how well they have adjusted initially to the forced change in their reality.

When attempts to reconcile the irreconcilable fail, as they must, dissociation is a way out, a way to reduce cognitive dissonance or unbearable conflict. When all elements are made conscious in therapy, the individual must learn to live with "all of the above" without feeling the pressure of forced choice and without recourse to defensive splitting apart, that is, to dissociated self-states. The task is as much cognitive as emotional, if not more so, for ultimately it is being able to put what they experience into the words that enables individuals to tolerate what was once intolerable.

Just as dissociated self-states and their multiple relationship conflicts are sure to interfere with the ability to make a satisfactory love relationship in adult life, certain behavioral symptoms also interfere with the individual's ability to form a lasting interpersonal relationship. Some symptoms that are a manifestation of early abandonment experiences and the core relationship problems that ensued are discussed in the following chapter.

Chapter Nine

Cherchez la Mère

Disturbances of Object-Seeking Behavior in the Wake of Early Abandonment Experiences

From Harry Harlow to Ronald Fairbairn, whether working with primates or humans, investigators have established the priority of object seeking over gratification seeking. The baby rhesus monkey gulps down the milk provided by a wire "mother" and then scrambles to the cuddly comfort of its terry cloth "mother." Apart from cases of infantile autism the human baby is attachment seeking from the start of life. In his monumental work on attachment and loss, Bowlby (1960) concluded that there is no rage as great as that evoked by the experience of abandonment.

Abandonment experiences may be chronic and repetitive, the outcome of inconsistent or ambivalent mothering. They may be sudden and total, as with the death of the mother or the departure of a beloved nursemaid. The sense of abandonment may also emerge long after the fact, as when a child learns she has been adopted and establishes, in her fantasy, a tie to her biological mother as well as feelings about having been given away. Abandonment may also become an issue when an older sibling who has played an important emotional role in a small child's life leaves for college or to get married, though the effect on the younger child will to an important extent depend on the age at which abandonment became an issue.

When the therapist is alert to data that abandonment was a significant factor in the person's formative years, he is more likely to be alert as well to the symptoms and behaviors that can be understood as the result of the meaning the child attached to being left, the feelings and fantasies that were stirred up at the time, as well as later attempts to cope with the emotional trauma. This chapter examines some important examples of these symptoms and behaviors.

Don Juan Behavior

As an example, *Don Juan behavior,* although relying on the individual's ability to sexually seduce and so to capture his object, has less to do with sexuality than with an obsessive need to magically undo the powerlessness of childhood and to prove he can capture his mother, along with undoing the anxiety, shame, and rage at that powerlessness. As a man this person is not interested in the object once he has won her. He must go on again and again, proving to himself that he *can* get her. In addition, although sex may be the vehicle for his conquest, by getting the woman to *desire him,* he can deny his own wish for the mother figure and abandon and frustrate the woman in a kind of vengeful enactment of the way he felt abandoned when he was young.

Proving his sexual prowess is not the aim. Rather, the core relationship problem vis-à-vis the mother is at the bottom of his way of being in the world and has to be confronted, teasing it out from its sexualized context. As a patient he may be adept at interesting the therapist in him in such a way as to project the desire for the connection into the therapist, denying his own wish. If the therapist inadvertently colludes with this dynamic, the individual can leave having once again proven to himself that he can capture the object and taking some pleasure in the retaliative aspect of his quitting therapy.

Fetishism

Another example of the pathology of the object-seeking process itself (as compared to a pathological way of relating), is *fetishism.* The early loss of the mother through death may lead to a number of restitutive fantasies and obsessions that both express the intense wish for her and a denial of the pain of the impossibility of the wish. A small boy's visual memories of mother may focus on her legs inasmuch as his child's stature put her legs at his eye level. As an adult he is not really able to remember her face. He becomes obsessed with finding a woman with perfect legs but is unable to find one who can live up to his standards. In fact *no* legs will be the right ones. He may even fall in love, but then the imperfection of her legs spoils the relationship for him. Only *mother's* legs (and mother with them) would be able to relieve him of the impacted grief of a lifetime and the guilt that he had in some way been re-sponsible for her disappearance. An attempt in therapy to question the basis of his choice of a woman is experienced as a threat to his restitutive fantasy. Therapy is a danger to be avoided.

Fetishism is regarded as a sexual perversion in which genital discharge requires the presence of the fetish. Usually, the fetish is a part of the body or some object belonging to or associated with the love object. In the past, instinct theory played a major role in the understanding of fetishism. Greenacre (1955) noted that it is the period of the transitional object (Winnicott, [1951] 1975) that is the first disturbed one for the fetishist and the vulnerable phallic phase that is the second period of traumatic disturbance. She writes that "the changeability from feelings of possessing a strong penis to feelings of not having any, occur with great rapidity" (p. 192).

Although Greenacre gives a nod to the object relations contri-bution of Winnicott, castration anxiety still has a central focus in her thinking. However, a fetish obsession may contain a more com-plex relational dynamic. The insistence on big breasts as a prereq-uisite for choice of partner has been found to conceal underlying relationship problems going back to when the child felt both trapped within and excluded from the marital triad. Having to ob-serve parental sexual involvement, he experienced impotent rage at being stimulated and frustrated. Now, the big breasts of his fe-male partner lure other men who then envy him his possession of the woman. His own impotent rage is projected into the anony-mous rival in a role reversal in which he identifies with the father who triumphed over him, and thereby he regains a sense of power. He refinds the alluring mother and retaliates against the father.

A countertransference blindness to the need for exploring what might seem to be an ordinary erotic preference (for big-breasted women) may arise when the therapist unquestioningly accepts this preference as a cultural ideal. However, when a single attribute is more important than an emotional, relational connection, whether that attribute be a fetish or an obsession, exploration of the individual's underlying relationship problem is required.

The Wish for Power over the Object

The wish for power over the object can be carried to the ultimate extreme. In his classic study of murderers, Bjerre ([1927] 1981) wrote of their hate: "It was the hate of the weak, suffering, and incompetent for all strong, happy, self-assured persons: it grew out of fear and envy, and in the last resort out of a sense of helplessness and inferiority, a consciousness of unfitness for the struggle of life." He noted that their "sense of powerlessness and inferiority in the presence of all human beings without exception" was the preeminent destructive force within them. He described how their sexuality could not be tied to any conception of love, and wrote of one notorious killer that "his pleasure in every new sexual connection was based on the imaginary belief that his mistress of the moment was completely in his power and that she must yield, even to the point of death, to his all-conquering whims" (p. 117).

Macdonald (1986) reports the statement of a man with necrophiliac fantasies: "He described with relish the feeling of power and security that he could enjoy in making love to a corpse; it is there when wanted, you put it away when finished with it, it makes no demands, it is never frustrating, never unfaithful, never reproachful" (p. 174). In short, we might say in self-psychology terms, it is the perfect selfobject, condensed with sexuality. It is the perfect mother of symbiosis, the good breast, with no life, or will, or desire of her own.

With both Don Juanism and fetishism (and perhaps with necro-philia in the extreme case), we have examples of the way in which sexuality captures, as it were, the core relationship problem and in so doing depersonifies it. *The thread of emerging sexuality becomes con-densed with the thread of object relations development. The original object seeking is now disguised as sexual gratification seeking and becomes equally all consuming.* In my view the analytic work depends on our ability to repersonify the conflict, to free it from its captor and address the dif-ficult work with respect to the core relationship problem.

The small child will do his best to find a way to capture his mother if she does not lend herself to his desired connection with her. Perhaps through trial and error he may come upon the solution of seduction, albeit not sexual at that age, or intimidation, or bribery, or ingratiation—one of any number of behaviors that will get her involvement if not her love. These dynamically motivated strategies are not the same as the false self, which is a charactero-logical adaptation to the mother whose own needs take precedence over the child's. Moreover, the learned behaviors aimed at captur-ing mother will be brought into the relationship with the therapist at the very start of treatment. Underlying this pattern is a trans-ference assumption that the therapist is like mother and will be available only through the same devices. In general, *pathology of object-seeking behavior itself* will lead to a failure to connect with the other in any meaningful way, a major problem in establishing a therapeutic alliance. It is important to cut through to the core rela-tionship problem as quickly as possible, to present the person's di-lemma and the inevitable price that is being paid as the old pattern continues to be acted out. Therapeutic failures generally occur early in treatment as just one more enactment of the individual's maladaptive solution to the conflict between wish and expectation of abandonment.

The early abandonment experience leads to core relationship prob-lems that interfere with making attachments, yet the first attach-ment, or connection, between patient and therapist may also be affected by the place of money in the therapeutic transaction. As a profession, psychotherapy entails receiving fees for the work. Conducting psychotherapy is, after all, how we make our living. The issue of money is there from the start of treatment. It is sometimes difficult to deal with the conflicts that may arise between us and the patient over payment of fees in a neutral manner. The patient's refusal to pay or denial of our worth hits us both personally and financially. Working with money issues in treatment is the subject of the next chapter, with attention to associated relationship problems.

Chapter Ten

Money Issues
and Analytic Neutrality

It is not likely that we can separate payment for psychoanalytic treatment from transference and countertransference. Freud ([1913] 1958) notes that the transfer of money is an integral part of the treatment, with possibly decisive consequences for the course of treatment. Although Kubie (1950) thinks that both therapist and patient should behave as if "money did not exist," it does in fact exist, and behaving as if it did not exist is in itself a stimulus to which the patient may be likely to respond. It is important to make the issue of money explicit, particularly when the core relationship problem is embedded within it.

Here, for example, is the case of a patient who always paid promptly, without being asked. Mrs. G. had been the family go-between in childhood, her parents going for long periods without speaking to one another. Every week her mother would ask her to go to her father to get the weekly household allowance check, and each week she would have to listen to his diatribe against her mother before he would have her write the check, which he would then sign. The asking for and receiving of money continued to be traumatic for Mrs. G. in her adult life. When her therapist told her that

The author gratefully acknowledges the permission of the publisher and editors to reprint this chapter, with slight adaptations, which was originally published in Sheila Klebanow and Eugene L. Lowenkopf (eds.), *Money and Mind*, pp. 175–181. Copyright © 1991 by Plenum Publishing Corp., New York.

he did not send bills but that the patient was expected to pay at the last session of each month, Mrs. G. found a way to avoid a replication of the original situation. At the beginning of every last session of the month, she set her prewritten check down on the corner of the therapist's desk. She said nothing and neither did he. Both behaved as if money did not exist. This avoidance led to the failure of the treatment to deal with her money anxieties and her underlying chronic trauma of being torn between warring parents.

In his pleasure at having a patient reliably and unconflictedly paying the bill, the therapist may inadvertently collude with the patient's denial that the exchange of money is part of the therapeutic transaction. To remind both of the reality, the therapist need only acknowledge receipt of the check, perhaps as simply as by saying, "thank you."

Freud refers to *psychoanalytic mechanics*, the kind of transactions dictated by the society in which we live. I see among these mechanics the pragmatics of money in the analytic situation.

Confrontation with the inescapable realities of life—death, taxes, and the therapist's bill—will certainly mean different things to different people. When we speak of maintaining the therapeutic frame (Langs, 1976), which must include the exchange of fees, we cannot assume that this frame is inherently neutral. It may be a challenge to the patient's overtly or covertly held illusions of specialness, in which case the need to pay a fee constitutes a *narcissistic wound*. Narcissistic wounds are never neutral, in spite of the patient's capacity to endure them without overwhelming shame or paranoia.

The pragmatic aspects of billing and collecting will be taken in and processed in accord with the patient's character structure, with his or her internal object relations setup as it is manifest in the complexities of here-and-now relationships. Preexisting defenses and coping strategies aimed at maintaining narcissistic equilibrium will be brought to bear. This will be as true of the repression of the neurotic patient as it will be of the splitting of the more primitively organized character disorder. Even in those instances where the payment of a fee is a relief to the patient who characteristically and cynically wonders what interpersonal price will have to be paid in important relationships, something is effectively hidden by the frame itself. As it did in the case of Mrs. G., the frame prevents the emergence of the conflict within the transference, whereas attention to it will lead to useful exploration of the embedded core relationship conflict.

A Variety of Meanings Attach to Payment

In his discussion of the payment of fees, Eissler (1974) makes it clear that no general statements can be made, that the specific meanings to specific patients will cover a wide spectrum of effects. A wealthy patient who is charged a high fee may see this as further evidence that he is sought after only because of his money or that if you have anything people will be out to exploit you. We might wonder how he felt emotionally exploited by his needy or narcissistic parent. In contrast another wealthy patient may not believe she is getting optimal service unless she pays a corresponding fee. We might learn that she felt emotionally abandoned when she did not meet with her mother's demands.

The therapist's approach to financial arrangements with patients is likely to be multiply determined. Issues such as prevailing peer community standards will enter in as well as the therapist's own issues of competition, envy, or masochistic self-denial with respect to peers. The therapist may gain superego gratification by not being as "greedy" as those peers. In moral masochism (see Chapter Sixteen) the sense of self as good is maintained by renunciation of desire. The secret moral superiority compensates for the shame of being victimized and taken advantage of in some relationship. The therapist's relation to money and what meaning it holds for him symbolically and dynamically will also be factors. Professional ego ideal and social values will certainly play a role. Countertransference issues may be indistinguishable from social values, and they may both be active within a single clinical situation.

Say, for example, that a therapist holds values relating to help-ing certain individuals who would be denied treatment unless they were assigned a greatly reduced fee. It is not unlikely that a judg-ment as to the worthwhileness of the patient enters into a decision to make such an offer. Already the dynamics are becoming com-plicated. Having made this offer, the therapist feels good about himself insofar as he is living up to his values. He will then be taken aback if the patient reports that he feels humiliated by the offer or burdened by it, feeling he has to make the financial sacrifice up to the therapist by making the therapist's work pleasant or easy. The patient may also be suspicious of the therapist's motives and won-der what will be asked in return. Instead of trust being generated, it is shaken. The therapist may feel wounded, his altruism having been misunderstood or unappreciated.

Eissler writes of the benefits for every analyst of seeing at least one patient without fee. In addition to the social benefits, he writes, it enables the analyst "to accumulate experience from analyses in which the fee factor plays no role as a motivating force (either in the patient or in the analyst) and should . . . [also] contribute to the refinement of the psychoanalytic technique." Given a society in which the patient surely knows that the payment of a fee is usual and customary, I do not understand how Eissler reasons that money, in its very absence, will not be a significant factor in the therapeu-tic relationship. Because the payment of a fee is a defining aspect of the professional as compared to the personal relationship in West-ern culture, Eissler's suggestion opens the door to a patient's assump-tion that her wishes for something unique and personal between her and her therapist have indeed come true. In such a case reality test-ing may be lost and a psychotic transference engendered.

The Importance of Analytic Neutrality

This all goes to say that practical day-to-day decisions about money matters in the therapeutic relationship are never simple matters of policy. Yet policy decisions are required regularly in any therapist's practice. Assuming that the therapist is for the most part aware of his own dynamics with respect to money, I would like to suggest a clinical principle to guide clinical decisions entailing payment or nonpayment of fees. This principle, simply stated, is that the therapist's policy decisions should not traumatize the patient and that the therapist should adhere as closely as possible to a stance of clinical neutrality in making those decisions. This, however, brings us to the question of what is neutral, and that will vary from patient to patient and from situation to situation.

For the answer to this question, I turn to Greenberg's creative and clinically useful definition of neutrality (1986), which allows us to apply neutrality in a manner specific and appropriate to the uniqueness of any given patient. Greenberg agrees with Schafer (1983) that there is an intimate connection between the therapist's neutrality and the patient's experience of safety, without which the patient would continue to "feel injured, betrayed, threatened, seduced, or otherwise interfered with or traumatized" (p. 95). In terms of a relationship model of psychoanalysis (as contrasted to a drive model), Greenberg notes that "the atmosphere of safety would depend on the analyst's ability to create conditions in which the patient perceives him as a new object." However, he adds, if the situation is too safe, there is no room for transference and for confronting the threatening feelings that are part of an archaic relationship. Neutrality embodies the goal of establishing an optimal tension between the patient's tendency to see the analyst as an old object and capacity to experience the analyst as a new object (p. 97). Greenberg writes: "The patient can become aware that he is assimilating the analyst into his world of archaic internal objects only when he has already become aware that there is an alternative possibility. . . . If the analyst cannot be experienced as a new object, analysis never gets under way; if he cannot be experienced as an old one, it never ends" (p. 98).

The closer our payment decisions can come to being true clinical decisions based upon our understanding of the patient's character structure and dynamics, the less likely we are to act out our countertransference motives through these decisions even when counter-transference issues are operating. The principle of neutrality provides us with a secure frame within which we can operate with relative equanimity and within which the patient and the clinical process are protected from serious therapeutic errors.

The Problem Patient

One man had two long-term therapies before coming to see me. The first entailed a dual-role situation in which he was both a patient and a student assistant to his therapist. He never paid the bill, despite many arguments about it, and the relationship ended with an accumulation of many thousands of dollars owed the therapist. The patient had almost exclusively negative feelings toward this former therapist. He felt entitled to free treatment because of the special nature of the relationship. His second therapist had been a woman who did not charge him above what his insurance paid, supposedly out of a stance of supporting his growth and professional maturation. His feelings toward her were predominantly positive.

The patient was established with a respectable income when he came to me. Although other factors were operative, the therapy bogged down because, for the first time in many years of treatment, he would have had to pay money out of his own pocket for therapy. His sense of specialness and entitlement, iatrogenically reinforced, did not yield to interpretation. His rage at having to pay seemed to him to be too realistic to be interpreted as a transference issue connected to his previous therapy experiences. He used the money issue, together with the humiliation of having to be in treatment at all, to justify ending treatment.

Eissler refers to the patient who believes he is so remarkable that he is not only entitled to free treatment but deserving of it. For such a person paying a fee constitutes so grave a narcissistic injury that he will not be able to start analysis. Therefore Eissler advises taking him into treatment without pay, anticipating that after adequate analysis the patient will be willing to compensate the analyst.

However, Eissler also notes that "it is advisable at this point to turn him over to another analyst, inasmuch as the transference situation has become too involved to be disentangled; moreover, as a result of the analyst's initial willingness to comply, the transference has become too libidinized to warrant any expectation of a promising course of treatment."

The iatrogenic complexities of this maneuver boggle my mind.

With 20–20 hindsight, I now wonder how treatment might have gone if I had started with my patient with a brief therapy contract that focused on payment for treatment. If this approach were successful, the humiliation of dependency on the therapist would be minimized, insofar as brief psychotherapy aims at avoidance of a dependent transference through its specific techniques of once-a-week face-to-face treatment, a time limit, and constant attention to dissolution of the transference by interpreting it within the focus whenever it emerges. The situation would have been more neutral because the patient would not have been faced with becoming a dependent hostage to a powerful object who only took from him, leaving him depleted and impoverished. Thus he might have been able to experience me as a new object. Yet he would also have experienced me as an old object insofar as I did indeed want *something* from him, namely my fee. The core relationship problem in this instance was the emotional exploitation he had experienced vis-à-vis an infantile, borderline mother, along with the danger of having to expose his dependency yearning toward her either to her or to himself.

With a theoretically sound clinical rationale informing my decision with respect to payment of a fee, I would not feel that I had been caught up in the rigid position of being unwilling to work without a fee, whatever the justification for doing so. Nevertheless I did not allow myself to be bullied into submission to his demands nor manipulated with guilt into acceding to them. Had I submitted, I would have found myself in the same position with him as he had been with his mother, the victim of a rageful, exploitative other. I would have colluded in this malignant reenactment. A brief therapy focus would have brought this dilemma out in the open to be worked with.

There are many situations that come up around the payment of fees, such as payment for missed sessions, third-party payment, raised fees, reduced fees, and bills allowed to accumulate. Taking the maintenance of analytic neutrality as a guiding principle, we cannot make across-the-board statements about any of them. When we try to do so, we inevitably get caught up in our own beliefs, values, and needs and our rationalizations of them or in theoretically narrow concepts that inevitably do a disservice to one patient or another. Other elements that may not seem as prone to evoke transference reactions nevertheless may do so, such as having a secretary conduct the business end of one's practice or mailing bills and checks with the result that no hand-to-hand exchange of money takes place.

In Eissler's comprehensive discussion of the payment of fees, it is clear that from time to time he turns to personal values and standards to support clinical judgment. He is not aware of this when he writes: "It may cause unnecessary pain to a patient to be told that it is for economic reasons that he is being refused analysis by a therapist by whom he wishes to be treated. It may be preferable, in such a case, to give 'lack of a free hour' as the excuse. Here, however, I am uncertain about the extent to which my suggestion is influenced by personal idiosyncracies."

When I have taken this very approach, I have found myself faced with a patient who then insists on waiting until I have a free hour. Even an excuse does not shield the individual from a narcissistic wound and envy of those for whom the therapist does have time. Furthermore, with the more primitive patient in particular, a relationship with the therapist forms in the patient's mind as soon as that patient accepts the referral and makes the initial phone call. With it the dependency is established, and the person will choose waiting over loss of the as yet illusory relationship.

Eissler also turns to his considerable past experience as a guide, yet there may be pitfalls for the therapist who makes a clinical decision based on someone else's past experience alone, even someone as eminent as Eissler. The idiosyncratic nature of analytic work requires a metaguide, a theoretical rationale for the moment-to-moment decisions that must be made about the pragmatics of money in the analytic situation. Knowing that judgment as to what is or is not neutral for a given patient will not be infallible, I still view neutrality as the most reliable principle on which to make these decisions.

In addition to attitudes about money and embedded core relationship problems, individuals' philosophy and values and their religion and politics are also part of who they are. These issues will inevitably arise in the clinical situation, sometimes as minor issues and sometimes as major ones. It is important not simply to accept them as givens but to understand embedded relationship problems in them as well. These topics are discussed in the next chapter.

Chapter Eleven

Religion, Values, and Clinical Issues

The question of values has been debated for centuries. The ancient philosophers argued the question of the highest good. Socrates said it lies in the objective fulfillment of a human need and not in the feelings of pleasure that accompany the process of desire and gratification. Aristotle believed that happiness is man's highest good and that happiness is attained through the satisfaction of all human needs and through the perfection of all of man's natural faculties. Spinoza, in contrast, called for a triumph of reason over emotion, for freedom from bondage to the passions.

Anthropologists' concern for values lies in the influence of the cultural value system on social behavior. Opler (1956), who attempts to synthesize the findings of anthropology with those of psychiatry, notes that cultural attitudes toward infancy and childhood, kinds of kinship settings, and values of human individual worth affect the handling and discipline of the infant and parental behavior and functioning. Despite his interest in the individual results of this constellation of factors, his view is that of the anthropologist— parents act as agents of their culture, and through them cultural values come to influence the personality of the child.

Alexander (1953) views cultural constellations as reinforcing and bringing forth certain emotional mechanisms. He writes: "Cultural factors as they appear in the methods of child-rearing and in parental attitudes undoubtedly have a great influence on the child's readiness to accept the process of maturation. But also the individual attitudes of the parents have an equally powerful influence." Alexander points out that there are both overprotective and rejecting mothers in every culture, "although either type may be the rule in one and the exception in another civilization." In essence he believes in "the overwhelming significance in personality development of the specific character traits of the parents and their relations to each other and to their children," observing that "cultural environment accounts only for certain similarities in persons of the same cultural group. For the tremendous individual differences among human beings living in the same group, constitution and the specific human influences are responsible."

Erikson (1943) came to the conclusion that "systems of child training . . . represent unconscious attempts at creating out of human raw material that configuration of attitudes which is (or once was) the optimum under the tribe's particular natural conditions and economic-historic necessities."

Now we are seeing calls for a return to "family values," after decades of fallout from the cultural rebellion of the 1960s and its "if it feels good, do it" philosophy and from the attitudes and behaviors of the 1970s, which came to be characterized as the me decade. Faced with the current focus on multiculturalism in our society and the inevitable questions that arise in doing the work of a psychotherapist, I go to my own dissertation (Horner, 1965) ("An Investigation of the Relationship of Value Orientation to the Adaptive-Defensive System of the Personality"), written over thirty years ago, and to what I noted then. "The current controversy over the role of values in psychotherapy and what therapists should do about it seems to assume a certain discontinuity between the value system and other aspects of personality with which we are more traditionally concerned in psychotherapy. Before one can come to any sound conclusions about the role of values in psychotherapy, the role of the value system within the individual must be examined more closely" (p. 3). I still subscribe to that point of view. From the results of my study, I concluded that values are indeed important considerations in psychotherapy, not as barriers to therapy but as significant dimensions in the dynamics of the personality. I found that stated goals and values often arise out of the needs, conflicts, experiences, defenses, and adaptations of the individual in accord with his or her unique life situation. From the perspective I am describing in this book, each of these values and goals will have an interpersonal, relational matrix within which it operates.

Values and Psychotherapy

Though we need to be aware of and learn about the values of any culture that is brought to us by our patients, the question of culture is still a psychological one. If we get side-tracked into the sociopolitical issues of culture, we are no longer acting as psychotherapists. Exploration of the cultural values and the individual's psychological relationship to them is part of the work. So often we find in immigrant groups a culture conflict experienced by the younger members of the group as they are exposed to the cultural values of the established peer group and of movies, television, and advertising. It is a conflict that is most painful when it is brought into the younger members' relationship with members of the older generation who reject the culture of their new surroundings. It is no different from the generation and culture conflicts of earlier waves of immigrants, and it is important that the therapist maintain a stance of neutrality so that the individual can come to grips with his or her dilemma in a healthy and constructive way.

Religious Issues

Whether the therapist is an atheist, an agnostic, or a devout believer and whatever her philosophical-psychological stance vis-à-vis the psychology of religion and religion's role in history, to impose either the therapist's doubts or her convictions onto the therapy is a blatant failure of neutrality and a violation of the patient's boundaries. Psychoanalysts may have a greater tendency than other people to agree with Freud's view of religion as essentially an obsessional neurosis. He

wrote ([1927] 1961c) that people's "acceptance of the universal neurosis spares them the task of constructing a personal one" (p. 44). If
a therapist agrees with this perspective, she will have to be careful
not to insinuate that belief into her interpretations and formulations. If that avoidance is not possible, it may be questionable
whether it is possible for that therapist to work with someone for
whom religion and spirituality are important. Religion can certainly
be used in the service of an individual's neurosis, and where that is
the case, it needs to be explored. But it is my view that as therapists
we have no right—if we do indeed believe that to be religious at all
is a manifestation of neurosis to be done away with—to work with
these patients.

On top of considering the individual's specific theological beliefs, the therapist can also consider the individual's relationship
with God, which is essentially an object relationship in its own
right and will be as subject to transferences as is any other relationship. When that relationship is a troubled one, it can be as
painful for the individual as a troubled relationship with a parent
or with a lover. Listening for manifestations of the conflicted setup
may reveal aspects of the individual that were heretofore hidden.

Knowledge of the individual's specific beliefs helps with the
exploration of this aspect of his or her life. It is to be hoped that the
educated psychotherapist will have some fundamental knowledge
about all of the major religious groups. For example, we might hear
a fundamentalist Christian patient state that she is sure that God
must hate her, and we might wonder what there is about her that is
so bad that God would feel this way. Knowing that belief in "God's
grace" is part of her religious belief, we might ask even more precisely what there is about her that is *so* bad that she is not as deserving of God's grace as everyone else. Her badness must be worse than
everyone else's. This could lead to an uncovering of the darker side
of the personality that the patient has kept hidden thus far.

Ultimately, God should be as freed from negative transference
as we hope the therapist will be. Whatever spiritual beliefs the indi-

vidual has may then be a source of comfort and support. From this perspective we might say that God is the inheritor of the role of the good background object of infancy. Sometimes an individual who experienced serious mental or physical abuse throughout childhood but who had a decent symbiotic period in the first year can hold onto the residue from those long-forgotten experiences through her conscious faith in a loving God. It is a psychological resource whose value should not be underestimated.

Political Issues

We may have a patient who brings in political views, whether liberal or conservative. If this becomes a frequent theme, we have to look for the psychological importance embedded in the particular political issues. It is very easy for a therapist in this situation to lose a clinical stance and either to join with the patient if the therapist is in agreement or to argue with the patient if not, forgetting the purpose of the meeting. Or the therapist, in a valiant effort to stay neutral, may simply let the patient go on and on and say nothing. The therapist may justify this avoidance by saying he is allowing the patient to associate. But it is a dead end, because it stays at the political level and is not transformed to the psychological level. However, saying something like, "Let's see why this issue is such a burning one for you," brings the discussion back to the psychological aspect of the person's politics. (We may inadvertently discover the psychological aspect of our own politics as well.) Even if we tip our hand, so to speak, we can say, "Let's go back and take another look at what you were saying."

Whatever the complexity, conflicts, paradoxes, or defenses characteristic of a person's psychological makeup, ultimately that person is all of one piece. No arena operates completely independently of the rest, no matter how split off it may appear. To bring it all together is our challenge and what makes the work so endlessly interesting. The focus of this book has been, thus far, on the *patient's* core relationship problem. The next chapter addresses the effect of the *therapist's* core relationship problem and how it may hinder, to a greater or lesser degree, the therapist's ability to do the work.

Chapter Twelve

The Therapist's
Core Relationship Problem

Countertransference Resistance

From Freud ([1910] 1957a) on, it has been noted that psychological factors *in the analyst* may interfere with the treatment process. Freud wrote: "We have become aware of the 'counter-transference', which arises in him as a result of the patient's influence on his unconscious feelings, and we are almost inclined to insist that he shall recognize this counter-transference in himself and overcome it. . . . [W]e have noticed that no psycho-analyst goes further than his own complexes and internal resistances permit" (p. 144). This chapter describes the more recent views of countertransference.

Tansey and Burke (1989), in their overview of the literature, describe the *totalist perspective*. They define *countertransference* as the therapist's total response to the patient, both conscious and unconscious: "This 'total response' includes all the thoughts and feelings that the therapist experiences in reaction to the therapeutic interaction whether they are considered to be 'real' or 'neurotically distorted.' The totalist definition includes so-called objective countertransference reactions (Winnicott, 1949), which any therapist would likely experience in response to a patient in a particular context; it also includes what are considered to be the idiosyncratic reactions of the therapist arising from the therapist's own personal conflicts" (p. 41).

Tansey and Burke add that "the therapist is encouraged to treat all thoughts and feelings as potentially important sources of information about the interaction with the patient. Within the totalist perspective on countertransference, the therapist, far from seeking to become impervious to the patient's influence, strives to appreciate the ways in which he is being *acted upon* by the patient. . . . We view countertransference as an umbrella term encompassing the concepts of projective identification, introjective identification, and empathy" (p. 41).

In this definition, with which I agree, countertransference reactions, rather than standing in the way of the work, may in some cases be an important source of information about the patient and what she is acting out in the transference. And this information based on the therapist's countertransference may *further* the work if, of course, the therapist makes appropriate clinical use of it.

Characterological Issues

I attend here to a specific aspect of the therapist's personal psychology that may, across the board, slant the way in which she relates to patients or to a specific group of patients and that reflects her own core relationship conflict. The therapist's way of being in the world vis-à-vis others may be built into her character or activated only in response to certain kinds of stress in the relationship. In the first instance, clinical work as a whole will be compromised. In the second, only work with certain patients will be affected. In either case it behooves us as clinicians to be able to identify and understand our own core relationship problems and monitor their activation in the clinical situation. By now I hope that this book has helped the reader identify and articulate her or his own problem, whether or not it has been relatively resolved in personal therapy.

Countertransference Resistance

Earlier I defined transference resistance as the patient's way of relating that has as its aim to bring about a wished-for interaction or to prevent a feared interaction. It is a way to manage the therapist and the process. Countertransference resistance, in a parallel manner, may have the same aim in its attempt to manage the interaction. At an unconscious level the therapist relates to the patient *as if* the patient were the therapist's parental figure, and brings to the interaction archaic adaptations and defenses set up vis-à-vis the mother or father in childhood.

Fear of the Object's Narcissistic Anger

Fears of angering the narcissistic object may lead to rigidly adhered to empathy when confrontation or interpretation are indicated. This might be the kind of situation in which the therapist's preferred theoretical orientation seems to justify what is essentially countertransference resistance. The more psychologically evolved patient may even be annoyed by the unwavering empathy, feeling he is being talked down to, that the therapist is being condescending, and that he is not getting what he intuitively knows he needs from treatment. Paradoxically, this kind of empathy constitutes a gross failure of empathy.

Need to Justify Oneself to the Object

A core relationship conflict may lead to a defensive posture on the part of the therapist in which he always has to have an explanation, either to do away with the anxiety of mystification or as a way to justify feelings and behaviors to mother. Even when they are correct, these explanations or interpretations are likely to be badly timed or to be experienced by the patient as off the wall because no basis or context for the interpretation has been established previously. In this setup the therapist may be usurping the patient's autonomy or undercutting her ability to think things through herself. Winnicott (1971) writes that "it is only in being creative that the individual discovers the self," and he adds that "a patient's creativity can be stolen by a therapist who knows too much" (p. 57).

To therapists who worry about not having the right answer, I will say, "The answer is always in the patient. All you need to know is the right question to ask."

Pressure to Perform

In other situations the therapist may, out of her own core relationship conflict, feel a pressure to perform, to prove her value to the patient, as the child once did vis-à-vis the mother, or to justify taking a fee, so as not to seem greedy or selfish. She may find ambiguity and paradox, which are inevitable qualities of the human psyche, intolerable and may experience pressure to clarify and resolve, attributing the same discomfort to the patient.

Resistance to the Frame

The therapist may feel powerless to maintain an appropriate frame if it makes her feel too much like the rigid and controlling father she resented so deeply. In an overly permissive reaction formation, transference fantasies and wishes may become realized, in some instances leading to a psychotic transference in which the reality of the relationship is either lost or can be denied. The therapist may justify the looseness of frame with theoretical jargon about the value of providing a corrective emotional experience. For *whom*?!

Self-Effacement

The self-effacing therapist who grew up believing that his thoughts, feelings, and wishes did not matter, may find it difficult to accept how important he is to the patient. This therapist may be oblivious to transference dreams or feel guilty about asking for money, allowing large balances to build up. How the patient interprets this will be consistent with the patient's psychological makeup. In addition, sooner or later the therapist may begin to feel taken advantage of, evoking buried resentments toward his own exploitative parent.

Having to Be "Good"

In Chapter Sixteen, I note the overriding importance to the masochistic personality of maintaining a self-image as "good." The "dark side" has been split off and repressed, displaced, or morally justified, and healthy self-protective and self-expressive aggression is blocked. The therapist who must protect an ego ideal that is characterized by its goodness is likely to be blocked from the use of clinically appropriate aggression that is manifest in confrontation. No matter how careful and gentle the confrontation, it is inherently aggressive inasmuch as it is used *against* the patient's defensive strategies. This kind of therapist has no difficulty as long as she can be *supportive, validating,* or *confirming.* Unfortunately, validating infantile, narcissistic rage may reinforce it, validating the infantile claims and expectations as well.

Need to Be Acknowledged

With some patients the very awareness of the therapist as a separate individual has to be denied, because the existence of the other is felt to be a threat to the self. The patient holds onto a fantasy that the therapist is essentially an extension of herself. In cases like these, we recognize the individual's vulnerability and lend ourselves to functioning, in self-psychology terms, as a selfobject for as long as is necessary. A transference interpretation is experienced as an assault or abandonment and may be interpreted as a sign of the therapist's narcissism. Giovacchini (1972) describes the *existential annihilation* that the therapist may experience in working with this kind of individual.

The therapist who cannot tolerate this necessary annihilation may feel impelled to insist his presence be noted in one way or another—if not through a transference interpretation, then through some form of self-disclosure that is unconsciously motivated to remove the intense discomfort of the imposed nonexistence. The therapist's own felt need to have, at least, his existence mirrored, will get in the way of his ability to stay with the patient as the patient needs him to do. This therapist may do fine with a different kind of patient but will find it intolerable to work with this individual.

Authority Figures

A therapist's relationship to her supervisor can also be a source of clinical difficulties. Whether the therapist takes a stance of obedient compliance or oppositional defiance, the patient will pay the price. Sometimes, for example, the therapist may apply something the supervisor has suggested in a manner that ensures its failure. There is a secret pleasure in proving the supervisor wrong and in making the claim, "I did what you told me to do."

I have heard, "I wonder what Dr. Horner would do now," and realized that the therapist had renounced his or her capacity to think. The emotional and cognitive autonomy required to do optimal work can be compromised as a consequence of core relationship problems that arose at various stages along the developmental continuum. Leftover conflicts from the rapprochement phase can lead to anxiety over taking autonomous action. Unresolved oedipal strivings can lead to a competitive need to triumph over authority figures in general. The unresolved adolescent task of becoming one's own authority and dealing with the guilt at overthrowing the authority of a loved parent can also inhibit independent thought and action. An idealization of authority figures can have the same stultifying effect as can an idealization of special teachers and their pet theories.

When a therapist has any of these core relationship problems, therapy becomes a three-person situation where the presence of the invisible supervisor comes between therapist and patient.

Preexisting Issues for Both Patient and Therapist

With all the current discourse in the analytic literature that presents meta-meta-levels of abstraction about the minutest subtleties of the clinical interaction, at times we can no longer see the forest for the trees. Gedo (1996), for example, in his critique of Stolorow and Atwood's *Contexts of Being: The Intersubjective Foundations of Psychological Life*, notes that these authors "attempt to transpose self psychology into the camp of therapeutic schools that regard psychological life from a radically relativistic viewpoint, that is, only as a function of intersubjective transactions." And, he adds, "following in the footsteps of deconstructionist hermeneutics, they follow a postmodern epistemology based on the alleged hopelessness of attaining objectivity." He concludes, however, that "the intersubjective viewpoint arbitrarily overstates the influence of the interpersonal field on adult behavior" (p. 1243). Although, as Ingram (1993) notes, every relationship has its own unique and unreproducible quality—what Ingram calls the *signature* of the relationship—nevertheless the patient does come into the situation with a psyche that predates her entry into treatment. The therapist comes into the situation with a psyche that predates the meeting as well. Patient and therapist do not *cause* one another's way of being in the world no matter what is actually evoked within the hour. Peskin (1997), in his article "Drive Theory Revisited," notes the importance for psychoanalysis of maintaining a connection to the natural sciences and adds that "to divorce our theoretical endeavors from reference to our evolutionary origins and development creates a detachment which may serve to incubate theories of an overly ideal nature about ourselves" (p. 385).

To know ourselves, to monitor the activation of our own core relationship problems so as to not act them out, is our responsibility as therapists. Ultimately, our role is to help the patient come to the same level of self-awareness, in the hope that the patient will be able to move beyond the impasse attendant on his or her unresolved core relationship problem.

No matter how well analyzed we may be, our core relationship conflicts can be activated from time to time. I am tempted to use the analogy of the computer. We do not erase our relationship documents from our hard disk. They go into the recycle bin and stay there. Unlike the discarded documents on our computer, they are not items we might want to be able to retrieve, but return they will when we find ourselves in a clinical situation that endangers us in old ways we once felt endangered. Characterological defenses and postures will emerge, and we may not be aware this is happening, perhaps not until the patient reacts to something confusing in our way of being with him or her.

Just as a therapist's unresolved core relationship problems can interfere with the work in a general way, so certain aspects of his or her background can interfere in a more specific way. It is inevitable in our training that certain caveats, taboos, and guidelines will be built into our way of dealing with certain decisions with which we may unexpectedly be faced in the course of an hour. The next chapter continues the theme of turning away from rigid, doctrinaire thinking left over from relationships with teachers and supervisors and, instead, trying to understand and handle these unexpected situations from the perspective of the individual's core relationship problem.

Chapter Thirteen

Moments of Decision

What Do I Say? What Do I Do?

Less experienced therapists are sometimes confronted with a critical decision with respect to what to say or do in response to the patient at some given moment. They may be tempted to turn to rules they have read or heard in their training—always do this or never do that—forcing the patient into a Procrustean bed. What is an appropriate response for one person may seriously backfire with another. The therapist's ability to articulate, at least to himself or herself, the patient's core relationship problem will provide a useful guide when these moments occur. Thus this chapter examines some issues of character assessment and some specific areas of clinical decision.

In both the little and big crises that arise in any therapy, the guiding information will come from what we know about the individual. A clear picture of the core relationship conflict and its developmental origin, of the developmental stage at which the person was psychologically derailed, of the subsequent elaborations of the conflict, and of the various adaptations and defenses that evolved in order to cope with what went wrong early on will enable the therapist to respond appropriately and effectively to the specific individual. Not only vulnerabilities but also strengths and resources must also be taken into account.

Kohut (1977) makes the distinction between the primary structures that evolve within the context of the relationship with the primary caretaker of infancy and the compensatory structures that in part make up for the failures of that first caretaker and that evolve within the context of the relationship with the father and other significant figures. These later structures contain strengths and resources that can make all the difference in the person's ability to do the work of treatment.

It is useful to set out consciously to develop this kind of profile for each new patient. Obviously, for some the picture will come to light readily; for others, not. But the diligent therapist will try to fill in the blanks as the work progresses. Sometimes the needed information actually comes as a result of an error, an assumption of strength that is not there, a misreading of the person's level at the moment. Sudden regressions carry with them a cognitive regression as well, and words, language, and logic that are usually available may fail the patient. Such sudden shifts in levels of organization may lead to failures on the part of the therapist to perceive the shift and to adapt his vocabulary and syntax to the patient's ability to hear and process interpretations or formulations at that moment.

These failures disclose the patient's vulnerability, that which triggers the regression, and reveal underlying material that is crucial to the treatment. More of the blanks are filled in, and a broader understanding of the individual results.

Gratification

One issue that comes up with some regularity in my consultation is that of *gratification*. The therapist may become anxious if he thinks it may gratify the patient if, for instance, he calls her after receiving a somewhat vague phone message from her. One of the most useful discussions apropos of this concern is the article by Myerson (1981) in which he points out the distinction between *need* and *desire*, or *wish*. In terms of treatment we have to ask whether our active response to the patient's passively felt need will enhance the ego through our function as a selfobject or whether it will infantilize the patient by reinforcing passivity and by giving credence to unrealistic wishes and fantasies. If we respond to desire, we gratify inappropriately. But if we do not respond to need, we traumatize the ego.

A patient who has an unresolved pre-oedipal conflict vis-à-vis the mother and who turned to the father as a substitute may sound quite oedipal as she speaks of her wish to be wanted by her father, a wish that she plays out as an adult with other men and that may be brought into the transference to a male therapist. As the result of the work, deeper mother issues emerge and the dependent yearning for the mother that had to be renounced so a premature pseudo-independence could take its place comes out with all the grief and despair of the true little girl self. After a disturbing message is left on the therapist's voice mail, he wonders if he should call her. On the one hand, if he does, will he be gratifying her wish to be special to her father, to have him show how much he wants her? Will this call set up false expectations about what the therapist does and does not offer? On the other hand, if he does not call, will he be abandoning the despairing child who cannot reach her mother? Will she give up, believing once again that there is something wrong with her, that it was her unreasonable neediness that drove her mother away? Which response at which moment? If we truly are unsure and have to risk making an error, I would choose the response that is least damaging and best amenable to remedying through later work. I would risk gratifying the wish inappropriately in preference to abandoning her in her need and precipitating a traumatic state.

The Empathy-Anxiety Gradient

Another decision may present itself. Do I make an interpretation, or do I function as an empathic selfobject? The same requisites for understanding will once again prevail—as they inevitably will. Many patients will shift self-states, and the therapist's ability to respond appropriately will depend on the his sensitivity to those shifts. Not only will the therapist modify the language he uses. He will also shift the therapeutic stance vis-à-vis the patient from self-object to separate other, from empathy to mild confrontation.

Bromberg (1980) refers to Sullivan's observations (1953) that the analyst must be responsive to where the patient is on a gradient of anxiety, trying to maintain that position at an optimally minimal level—low enough that the patient's defenses do not foreclose analytic inquiry, but high enough that the defensive structure itself can be identified and explored. Bromberg writes of the *optimal balance between empathy and anxiety as an approach to treatment that is independent of the analyst's personal metapsychology.* An in-depth understanding of the patient's way of being in the world and of the underlying conflicts will enhance the therapist's ability to perceive accurately where the patient is on this *empathy-anxiety gradient.* On one hand failures of empathy can upset the therapeutic alliance. On the other an overly empathic stance accompanied by a failure to confront and work with anxiety-laden issues may lead to a stalemated treatment.

Physical Contact

Another and not unusual moment of decision occurs when the patient wants a hug and moves toward the therapist at the end of the session. The whole issue of physical contact is, as we know, fraught with potential dangers, both psychological and legal. This discussion addresses the question from a clinical perspective.

Is the request for the hug prompted by an unrealistic and unarticulated wish to be specially loved, or will the hug help the patient quiet down an internal emotional state bordering on the traumatic? Will it enable him to leave the room, get in his car, and return to work?

Myerson's distinction between need and desire is certainly relevant here. There are times when the more fragile individual loses self-cohesion and reacts with panic. Sometimes words cannot help and a touch—perhaps a hand on the shoulder—prevents what seems to be an inevitable decompensation. This is a situation of need, not of desire.

One cannot push the patient away without severe narcissistic wounding and humiliation. A minimalist response that does not shame but also that does not encourage may be the best one can do at the moment. It will be important to explore the meaning of the wish for the hug at a later time, but again the potential for humiliation is great. The exploration may be a silent one in the mind of the therapist, and the timing of any actual discussion of the subject will require the therapist's tact, sensitivity, and thorough knowledge of what it will mean to the patient.

Sometimes it will be discovered that the hug expressed a wish for reassurance that the therapist was not angry because the patient had expressed negative thoughts or feelings, especially toward the therapist. This finding will open up a fruitful area of conflict. Generally, once this underlying issue is articulated the patient will no longer act upon the anxiety but will bring it into the work when it arises again. The absence of shaming and the gentle manner of the therapist will not lead to hurt anger and withdrawal. The request for the reassuring hug tends to disappear when properly handled.

One patient recalled a previous treatment when she tentatively verbally expressed a wish to be held. The work had focused on oedipal wishes, and her lifelong denied yearning for her mother had come to the surface. Because of a marital schism between her mother and father, to choose her father did indeed mean she had to renounce her wish for her mother. But the therapist responded harshly to her wish, saying, "The trouble with you is that you want gratification and not therapy."

It is no surprise that the earlier pre-oedipal conflict returned then to its hiding place until years later in a subsequent analysis. The patient then said she would have been very frightened if the therapist had acted to grant the wish. If, however, he had said gently, "Tell me about your wish," she would have been able to resolve the underlying conflict and come to grips with the emotions that troubled her in the here and now.

Whether it be a doctrinaire stance on the part of the therapist or a reaction to his own anxiety, this kind of error is too costly for the patient. Conversely, the holding response of a quiet, understanding nod may be all that is needed.

Timing of Interpretations

A common error is that of the therapist who moves in to ask about the transference implications of certain behaviors at the very start of the work, such as the patient's "misunderstanding" about the fee. Without a context, such inquiries are likely to be experienced as off the wall and are likely to abort the treatment before it begins. This is a moment when we should decide *not* to pursue what may be an underlying problem. Instead, the event may—or may not—be raised at some future time within the context of the core relationship conflict and how it becomes manifest in the here and now. For example, later on it might be on target to say something like, "Your fear of being taken advantage of has been here since we started our work, the fear that I might charge you too high a fee, just as the price you had to pay for your mother's love was too high. That fear and vigilance follow you everywhere."

Both jumping to conclusions and jumping the gun will lead to unnecessary and avoidable errors. *The therapist has to be able to tolerate not knowing and also knowing and keeping it to himself.* The common thread throughout all these moments of clinical decision is that of knowing the patient well enough in terms of her core relationship problem to know the meaning and effect of any intervention made or not made.

Gifts

We are likely to feel on the spot when the patient presents us with a gift. What do we do? The answer to this is itself a pair of questions: What will be the consequences of accepting the gift? And what will be the consequences of refusing it? How we answer these questions will depend on our understanding of this unique individual in relationship terms.

Refusal of a gift that is an expression of the patient's genuine gratitude can be devastating, not unlike the effect on a child of the mother's rejection of its offer of love. If refusal of the gift will be so narcissistically wounding that the therapeutic alliance will be damaged, it is better to accept the gift with a simple "thank you" and to hold off any discussion of it until a later time.

One patient believed that people liked him only because of what he did for them. For the first two Christmases, he bought me expensive gifts. I was absolutely sure he would equate the refusal of the gift as a refusal of him, as he also would have experienced my interpretation at that time. We worked on the need to pay his way and the wish not to be "beholden" until he was able to stop playing this out in his outside life. He came to realize I cared for him beyond the money I made from his fee. At that point he simply stopped bringing me gifts. I did not feel it was necessary to go back and bring up the earlier gifts because at that time it would have been experienced as a humiliation.

In two other instances, I did refuse gifts. When a young woman sheepishly handed me a package, it was clear that the gift was an attempt to bribe me into not being angry because she was going to take a trip and would miss our session. I said, "No, thank you," and made the interpretation, and it proved well that I did. I also refused a gift from a very disturbed man who was always on the brink of a psychotic transference. After an obviously expensive gift was delivered to me, I did not open it but simply said it was a matter of policy not to accept gifts from patients. I believed that this statement of frame was necessary as a reinforcement of reality.

In these instances the answers to What do I say? What do I do? came from an understanding of the individuals' core relationship conflicts and how they dealt with them.

The next section discusses working with a variety of especially difficult patients, once again from the perspective of their core relationship problems. This perspective helps us understand not only the difficulty but also how to approach working with it. The first of these difficulties is interminable therapy.

Part Three

Difficult Patients and Clinical Problems

Chapter Fourteen

Interminable Therapy and Transference Resistance

When we have been therapists for a sufficient number of years and have worked with men and women through long-term in-depth therapy, we become aware of certain individuals who never seem able to approach, much less carry through, a process of termination. They may even go from one therapist to another, never bringing treatment to a satisfactory conclusion. This state of impasse, in my experience, appears remarkably syntonic as these patients settle in, session after session, to what has become an intrinsic aspect of their lives. What we are likely to find is that the core relationship conflict has not even been identified, much less worked through, especially as it was played out in the transference.

Termination is a specific stage of the overall treatment process. As such it arises organically, evolving as a final phase of the work. The shift to this phase is generally noted by both therapist and patient. The *organic* termination stands in contrast to the *forced* termination, which comes about because of circumstances external to the treatment process or to the therapy relationship. It may result when the therapist moves away for example. Forced termination is common when third-party payers refuse permission for further treatment. *Traumatic* terminations are those in which the treatment is cut off because of a severe deterioration or disruption of the therapeutic alliance. This chapter addresses resistance to taking the final step of a treatment process that seems to be the inevitable next step.

In these days of managed care, with long-term treatment being the exception rather than the rule, the very concept of interminable therapy may puzzle the younger therapist. Nevertheless, an understanding of the underlying principles will be useful when terminations are forced upon us by economic necessity.

From Freud ([1937] 1964) on, the problem of interminable treatment has been considered from a variety of theoretical perspectives. Freud described the impasse in his account of his analysis of a young Russian man

> spoilt by wealth, who had come to Vienna in a state of complete helplessness. . . . In the course of a few years it was possible to give him back a large amount of his independence, to awaken his interest in life and to adjust his relations to the people most important to him. But there progress came to a stop. We advanced no further in clearing up the neurosis of his childhood, on which his later illness was based, and *it was obvious that the patient found his present position highly comfortable and had no wish to take any step forward which would bring him nearer to the end of his treatment. It was a case of the treatment inhibiting itself: it was in danger of failing as a result of its—partial—success* [p. 217, emphasis added].

A major form of transference that leads to impasse is transference resistance. Freud attempted to understand interminable analysis within the limits of his theory of the time, writing that "a constitutional strength of instinct and an unfavourable alteration of the ego acquired in its defensive struggle . . . are the factors which are prejudicial to the effectiveness of analysis and which may make its duration interminable" (p. 221). He added that instead of asking how cure comes about by analysis, we should ask, What are the obstacles that stand in the way of such a cure? As we come to understand more and more the centrality of interpersonal and relationship problems underlying the patient's difficulties, we can take that same approach with respect to interminable treatment. We will probably find that the core relationship conflict is the obstacle at the center of the transference resistance, which as I described earlier, is a patient's defensive way of relating to the therapist, a way of managing the therapeutic relationship so as to bring about a wished-for interaction or prevent a feared interaction with the therapist. This behavior may come out of anxiety or out of the dictates of character pathology.

Following is an example of such a situation.

Attribution of Narcissistic Vulnerability in the Therapist

Family therapists Boszormenyi-Nagy and Spark (1973) write of *invisible loyalties*, in which the needs of the individual stand in opposition to the needs of the multipersonal system. My concept of *loyalty* implies something freely given, so these invisible loyalties seem like a form of servitude in which the individual is bound not only by guilt but also by fear of the angry object along with anxiety over the potential destructiveness attendant on his or her own inevitable rageful resentment of this bondage.

In situations of apparently interminable treatment it is not uncommon to find in some situations that the individual grew up a hostage to the mother's or father's pride, to a parent's fragile self-esteem. In these instances the narcissistically wounded parent turned ragefully against the child. The child soon learned where parental vanity was invested and how to cater to that vulnerability by negating the aspect of self that threatened it. The problem might have arisen in playing games, all the way from the child's game of Chutes and Ladders, to Monopoly, to a tennis match. The father had to win, and the child learned to lose. Or the father always had to be the one who knows, so the child learned when it was not safe to know and how to turn to the father for his wisdom in order to puff him up and keep him in a good mood. Or perhaps the mother's opinion was challenged, and her rage sent the child into a fearful retreat from her own thinking. It is particularly the inhibition of thinking and knowing that becomes a barrier to the treatment process. The patient may act as though only the therapist has the right to think and to know. Although a good deal of ground may be covered and some minor progress achieved, the transference is burdened with the individual's assumption that the therapist, like the father, must be the one to know, must need to be puffed up.

A salient and unavoidable quality of the treatment situation is that the relationship is inherently hierarchical. No matter how humanistic or egalitarian the values of the therapist, in addition to the transferences the patient brings to the relationship, a built-in asymmetry is manifest in the reality that it is the patient who goes to the therapist's office, asks for help, and pays for the treatment. Whether we refer to *doctor* and *patient* or *counselor* and *client*, the asymmetry is there from the start. In the best of treatment outcomes this sense of asymmetry is largely if not almost completely dissolved by its end. The good termination should carry with it the dissolution or resolution of transference to a large degree, although it is likely that vestiges will remain. In many cases of interminable treatment, the transference resistance is a perhaps silent but unyielding structure.

Individuals in interminable treatment will often say something directly or act in a manner aimed at puffing up the assumed vanity of the therapist. This is not idealization—far from it. The patient may even feel a secret satisfaction in playing the therapist for a fool if she colludes with the charade. The therapist will often feel vague discomfort with this patient and not know why. Because of the lack of emotional presence and absence of authenticity, the therapist often will feel sleepy with these patients even though they may go on and on in a kind of parody of the free association process. The importance of not knowing and of having to lose in what is seen as intrinsically a competitive situation—as it was with the mother or father—leads patient and therapist both to a sense of futility despite their dogged perseverance. Buried deeper is the patient's angry resentment at the "rules" by which the self must lose and his or her corrosive envy of the one who has the right to win.

The key to ending the stalemate is a combination of interpretation and confrontation of the core interpersonal dynamic and how it is reenacted with the therapist. Until the issue is joined the individual may drift from one therapy to another, a kind of serial interminability. These therapies may each be of years' duration. The years of the patient's life and his or her limited financial resources are also eaten away. It is up to the therapist to confront the issue, as such individuals will not take the initiative or challenge the therapist.

Forced Termination and Confrontation of Impasse

It is interesting that Freud ([1937] 1964) envisioned the usefulness of time-limited therapy in the case of interminable therapy. He wrote:

> I have subsequently employed this fixing of a time-limit in other cases as well. . . . There can be only one verdict about the value of this blackmailing device: it is effective provided that one hits the right time for it. . . . [O]nce the analyst has fixed the time-limit he cannot extend it; otherwise the patient would lose all faith in him. . . . [T]he patient [may] continue his treatment with another analyst, although . . . such a change will involve a fresh loss of time and abandoning fruits of work already done. . . . [T]he decision [about the right time] must be left to the analyst's tact. A miscalculation cannot be rectified. The saying that a lion only springs once must apply here [p. 219].

In my own work doing brief therapy, I found its principles to be useful in bringing to a close long-term therapies that had bogged down because of a failure to address a major transference resistance related to the necessary *overthrow of the therapist*. If we set a termination date, allowing for a reasonable time to work this through and applying the principle of brief therapy, we are often able to bring the treatment to a constructive close. The time may be as long as a year, but the frame will make it possible to address the core relationship conflict that lies hidden in the endless treatment.

The especially relevant principle of brief treatment is the formulation of a focus and holding to it. In cases like those described here, *the focus will be the relationship impasse that exists in the transference and the core relationship conflict vis-à-vis the parent that underlies it.*

I have used the brief therapy format with people who have come to me with a history of many years of treatment with good therapists. I have made it clear that the treatment would be time limited and have begun with what made it necessary for them to stay in the role and identity of patient and how this related to the transference. In the case of an individual whose major connection to his mother was through his having been sick as a child, the very act of being in therapy was an enactment. In a case like this the person may combine the wish for sexual gratification with the necessity of holding to the role of the sick one and turn to sex therapists to play out the scenario with him.

These examples illustrate how the relationship rules of the family of origin may lead to the establishment of a transference resistance, and it is in this relational stalemate that the interminability is rooted.

By and large, any form of transference resistance, if not addressed directly in the analytic work, will lead to a stalemated situation. The situation can go on for many years if the patient finds comfort in the state of equilibrium, albeit an equilibrium resting on a pathological foundation.

Just as unidentified core relationship conflicts may underlie interminable treatment, so may they underlie the situation in which what appears to be progress in therapy seems to backfire. Why helping sometimes does not help is discussed in the following chapter.

Chapter Fifteen

When Helping Doesn't Help

The Negative Therapeutic Reaction

In this modern era of the computer, we have become aware of the mischief-makers whose playground is cyberspace. We have become familiar with the concept of the computer virus, a command planted in a program that upon a given stimulus will activate the program's self-destruction. The *negative therapeutic reaction* can be viewed as analogous to the computer virus. Until we are able to identify the core relationship conflict that is active in this kind of situation, we are likely to feel puzzled and helpless. We may even get angry at the patient, believing he is just trying to defeat us in some kind of power dynamic.

In the previous chapter the role of the core relationship problem in transference resistance is clearly manifest in the example of the individual who as a child was hostage to a parent's self-esteem. For this individual, a relationship taboo prevents the necessary overthrow of the therapist that will allow the individual to become her own authority. *The negative therapeutic reaction described in this chapter is a reaction against the work itself*, although the therapist will certainly be seen as the agent of the work and thus dangerous in her own right. *The work endangers something that must be preserved regardless of how problematic it is*, and a self-destruct mechanism is activated by that threat to the individual's uneasy homeostasis within the core relationship conflict.

Though both interminable treatment and the negative therapeutic reaction can be defined in broad general terms, when we get right down to a specific individual, we need to look at the specific relationship context within which these situations may occur. This context will vary from patient to patient. It is so important to remember that no two people are alike but are as distinctive as their fingerprints or DNA. This is why books such as this one can offer only a general guide for the direction of the work. There is no substitute for the clinical acumen of the therapist.

Freud described the "negative therapeutic reaction" in 1923, remarking that in the case of individuals who exhibit this reaction, "there is no doubt that there is something . . . that sets itself against their recovery, and its approach is dreaded as though it were a danger. . . . [T]he need for illness has got the upper hand in them over the desire for recovery. If we analyse this resistance . . . even after allowance has been made for an attitude of defiance towards the physician and for fixation to the various forms of gain from illness, the greater part of it is still left over; and this reveals itself as the most powerful of all obstacles to recovery" (Freud, [1923] 1961b, p. 49).

The Meaning of Help

Renik (1991) has stated that "the important point about a negative therapeutic reaction is not whether the patient's distress rises or remains constant, but that he experiences therapy as causing pain rather than relief, and that this experience remains unaltered by *apparently* valid analytic understanding of its determinants" (p. 88, emphasis added).

In the case example presented by Renik, the patient states that he needs "help" desperately. The word help cannot be glossed over and simply taken at face value. As a signifier (see Chapter Three) it may not mean the same thing to the patient as it does to the therapist. And even more likely, the patient may not know what kind of help he actually needs. A cry for some kind of relief from distress may touch our therapist's heart, motivating us to rush in with measures to ameliorate the distress, such as medication. This can constitute a major error, as I will describe in a later example. Therefore it may be useful to inquire—carefully, of course—what the patient means by help.

Renik cited Shengold (1979), who "makes the point that often the young victim cannot afford to register the noxious image of the abusing parent" (Renik, 1991, p. 96), and Renik noted that this patient's negative therapeutic reaction is a way of discrediting his own perceptions of his mother. An example of this in Chapter Seven describes how getting worse as a result of the work may take the form of somatic symptoms that at times can be almost disabling. Renik wonders if in many cases valid analytic work has not produced progress because a crucial aspect of the patient's resistance has been overlooked. He advises that the central analytic task in the kind of situation he is describing "is to interpret the denial in fantasy served by the patient's complaints." And he adds that "once this defensive function is clarified, it becomes possible to discern the traumatic transference for which the negative therapeutic reaction was a reassuringly counterfeit substitute" (p. 99).

Renik notes that virtually all writers about the phenomenon follow Freud in regarding the negative therapeutic reaction as primarily an expression of aggression. He expresses the opinion, which I share, that although aggression plays a role, he has never seen a negative therapeutic reaction resolved through work guided by a formulation centered on aggression. And I further agree with him that a focus on the object-preserving aims, rather than the destructive behaviors, of provocative and hard-to-treat patients is likely to be more productive and has a better chance of resolving the clinical impasse.

With the focus on the core relationship conflict or problem, we can more readily understand the downside of being helped and perhaps head off years of impasse with increasing levels of frustration and hopelessness in both patient and therapist. At the start of treatment we often ask why the person has come, how she wants us to help her. We have to be careful that our own definition of help (based either on theory or a rescuing countertransference) does not set up the potential for the negative therapeutic reaction at the outset.

The Danger of Loss

In Chapter One, I described the situation in which the patient tells us that the only attachment he has is to his depression and wonders if we can help him. I hypothesized two ways to understand this—that the failure of maternal responsiveness left him in a chronic state of anaclitic depression as a baby or that the mother's depression meant the only connection between them was in his joining her in that affect state. For this individual, depression can signify both object loss and object connection. We may also get a history of many failed therapies and so be alerted at the get-go to the possibility, as Renik (1991) warns us, that a crucial aspect of the patient's resistance was overlooked.

What happens in the treatment if, when he asks us if we can help, we assure him we are hopeful that he can be cured of his depression? What if, in our alarm, we say he should also be on antidepressive medication? Are we in effect telling him he should be cured of his connection to his primary object? And in addition, are we telling him we cannot tolerate the self that feels most real to him? Does helping mean getting rid of his depression, or do we have to join and connect with him in his most real and object-related state? Any action on our part aimed at making him "feel better" is far more likely to make him feel more despairing and hopeless.

Another not uncommon clinical issue is the individual's quasi-symbiotic tie to the mother. We may, in our therapeutic zeal, see as the goal of treatment helping him to *separate and individuate*. I recall some time ago hearing this approach referred to as *wedge therapy*. Jeopardy to the individual's connection with the object, and thus to the object and to the self as well, will make it necessary for the individual to block any treatment he experiences as aimed at breaking his bond-bind with the mother. The therapist's under-standing and articulation of the core relationship conflict, the in-evitable ambivalence toward connection, and the wish-fear dilemma will make it more possible to prevent an acting out against the treat-ment itself. I find it useful to articulate the dilemma the patient is in, caught in a kind of triangle between his mother and his therapist and the therapy. If he and the therapist define the treatment goal as becoming more autonomous, he will not only be disloyal to his mother, he might even be responsible for her failure to thrive. His "recovery" will mean her destruction. The strength of the dangerous anger and aggression that must be repressed will most likely be in proportion to the felt sense of paralysis resulting from the core rela-tionship conflict.

Resistance to Termination

As the work seems to have proceeded well and we move into the final phase of treatment that will culminate in termination, other dynamics and resistances come into play. Thus Loewald (1979) noted that the overthrow of parental authority and the assumption of responsibility for one's own life takes place developmentally along with the severing of the dependent ties of childhood, stating that "not only parental authority is destroyed by wresting author-ity from the parents and taking it over, but the parents, if the process were thoroughly carried out, are being destroyed as libidi-nal objects as well" (p. 757).

If the goal of therapy is to help the individual get a better sense of his own identity and goals for his life, he runs into the conflict of what abandoning his mother may mean. It may be tantamount to destroying her, from her perspective and now in his belief system also. If he individuates, he will experience unbearable guilt, fear about his destructiveness, and anxiety at the prospect of loss of his primary object, which leaves him depressed. When his survival and his mother's survival are mutually exclusive, what we deem progress in treatment will send him into dark and frightening places.

The wish to preserve or protect a parental figure will be manifest in the transference, and the individual will be loathe to overthrow the therapist. The therapy may shift into interminability unless this core relationship conflict is brought to the fore and worked with, both as it pertains to the parent and to the therapist. This is an example of a core relationship problem that may arise in adolescence in the context of a relatively healthy early development. Sometimes it may be an especially difficult struggle in the case of the son vis-à-vis a loved father. The patient may want to hold onto the therapist but now in the form of a mentor. The man who continues to seek mentors throughout adult life may be avoiding this task of adolescence.

The resistance that stems from the core relationship conflict is the "left over" aspect that Freud described as "the most powerful of all obstacles to recovery," regardless of where along the developmental continuum it may arise. In all of these difficult clinical situations, eventually the individual must confront his or her dark side if he or she is to be able to end treatment and to profit from it. Unresolved core relationship conflicts are central to the barrier to this confrontation.

In my years of acting as a consultant and supervisor, I have observed how often one of the most difficult to treat patients is the *good girl*. The work is not difficult because it is stormy, as is the case with some patients with more primitive problems and personality disorders. It is difficult because of the characterological defenses that operate to thwart the treatment process. The next chapter discusses the complexities of moral masochism.

Chapter Sixteen

The Masochistic Personality Disorder— A Diagnosis Worth Keeping

Working with the Good Girl and the Good Boy

In my years of work with therapists who found themselves at a therapeutic standstill with their patients, the most common thread to emerge has been the one I discuss in this chapter.

It is unfortunate that *masochistic personality disorder* has been eliminated from the *Diagnostic and Statistical Manual of Mental Disorders*. It has a place within what I view as a family of disorders, the members of which fall along a common developmental track. They are the paranoid personality disorder, the narcissistic personality disorder, and the masochistic personality disorder. I see each arising at a different point along the developmental continuum and each characterized by a history of a significantly salient or predominantly negative or hurtful caretaking environment. The later the derailment, the more the positive elements from earlier stages will contribute to the overall picture.

The *paranoid personality disorder* has at its core a salient persecutory object alongside an anaclitically depressed, objectless self. It is set in motion in the first year of life. There may be psychotic aspects as well, also of a paranoid quality. Because critical organization processes ought to take place in the first year of life, the effects of gross environmental failures or assaults during this period are the most severe and are basic to personality formation and disorder.

I see the *narcissistic personality disorder* as arising in the second year, with the onset of the rapprochement phase of development, and reflecting the inability of the child to bring together into a single representation images of the object that is experienced as alternately good or bad. That is, the parental inconsistency is so chronic and so emotionally traumatic, the child at this age is cognitively unable to bring the separate object images into a single albeit ambivalently loved other. The omnipotent grandiose self serves as a defensive fallback structure when the good object is disappointing and is devalued and discarded. Kohut (1971) describes this transference dynamic that shifts from an idealizing transference to rageful devaluation and the mobilization of the grandiose self. That is, the individual *splits* into all good or all bad. What distinguishes this splitting is that it is evidence of a developmental failure to integrate what, for the child, was unintegratable. The split we see in the masochistic personality is a defense against the intolerable conflict of ambivalence. We may see the further regression of the narcissistic personality to a paranoid structure when the grandiose self is challenged by adversity or by a therapist's overly aggressive interpretation.

As the child proceeds further along the developmental continuum to the third year of life, if the relationship with the primary caretakers is overly conflict ridden and inconsistent, perhaps with a combination of highly gratifying interactions and highly frustrating or hurtful ones, the child attempts to come to grips with an intense ambivalence, the conflict between love and hate toward the object. I see this failure of the caretakers to support the child's growing individuality and psychological autonomy as the masochist's point of derailment, the point at which the *masochistic personality disorder* arises. Hostility toward, rejection of, or abandonment of the little person the child is becoming leads to defenses and adaptations in the child that endeavor to preserve loving affect toward the object and to protect the good object from the rage and hatred that is felt from the negative side of the ambivalence. Keeping the self good and powerless functions toward this end. A defense against the shame that is felt as a result of taking on the devalued position vis-à-vis the powerful object can often be found in a secret superiority, usually a moral superiority. The associated contempt for the other who buys into the consciously played out self-effacing posture, along with the compensatory moral superiority, can be viewed as analogous to the devalued object–grandiose-self shift observed in the case of the narcissistic personality disorder. The self-effacing behaviors and the claims of unimpeachable goodness are manifestations of reaction formation.

There is, in the adult, a double projection. First she projects the narcissistic and rageful object into the other and then relates in a manner to appease and placate that person. Then her own repressed narcissistic rage, evoked by being forced to deny herself in the service of the other, is also projected. With both she caters to the narcissism she has attributed to the other, so the other will not turn against her. Then there is further resentment at being the one sacrificed to the wishes and demands of the other. It is a vicious circle that feeds on itself. It is in this piece of the circle— her own denied and projected rage—that we can see the familial resemblance to the narcissistic personality disorder. The angry feelings of entitlement to compensation for the self-sacrifice may come out in the form of stealing. She feels perversely justified and without guilt.

The masochistic personality has one foot in the pre-oedipal stage and the other in the oedipal stage and may often be seen as more evolved than she is. Elsewhere (Horner, [1979] 1984) I referred to this position as *pre-neurotic*. Whatever the characteristics of neurosis, there are also characteristics of a character disorder. Nevertheless, the relationship advancement to the capacity for ambivalence and associated cognitive achievements in this individual may make it more possible for us to do straightforward interpretive work than we can in the more primitive constellations. Even when getting to the dark side, the therapeutic alliance is not damaged, and the observing ego can be relied on in the work.

The use of more primitive defense mechanisms—denial, introjection, and projection—speak to the failure to evolve fully into what is characterized as a neurotic structure. The use of repression that is part of the reaction formation and of rationalization are evidence on the side of higher functioning.

What I have observed clinically is the overarching importance of preserving an image of the self as good. There is a transformation of what is bad—that is, the more primitive hate and rage—into a morally justified, self-righteous position, with anger coming out in the form of righteous indignation. The word *moral* in *moral masochism* is most apropos. Even the defensive superiority has moral overtones. The dark side where rage, hatred, and envy dwell is harder to get to in the analytic work. Enormous affect and energy can be mobilized around social or political causes, where the overdetermination of both is evident. Displaced in this way, aggression can be morally justified, as in a wish to be able to fight and kill as a soldier in a just war. Uncovering the demons and monsters, however, is essential to a successful therapeutic outcome. The capacity for healthy self-assertive, goal-oriented behavior will inevitably be tied to what is repressed. Desire and will belong to the repressed and frustrated self. This exploration is not likely to be without high levels of fear and guilt and will be the most strongly resisted area of work. Dreams are often revelatory, but the work on them tends to slip away. It brings both the patient and the therapist face-to-face with the repressed negative parental imago and the feelings and impulses associated with it. There may be corresponding dissociated self-states as well (see Chapter Eight). Under certain circumstances this setup may take a malignant turn.

Malignant Regression

The movie *Primal Fear* presented the transformation of frightened, humiliated Aaron into murderous, contemptuous Roy. Put forth as a case of multiple personality disorder, it shocks the audience at the end with evidence that Roy knowingly hid behind the persona of innocent victim Aaron. Aaron's mother had died when he was twelve, leaving him with a brutal father who both humiliated and terrorized him. The stuttering boy hid his dark side well until he received a later traumatic humiliation at the hands of another father figure, whom he also professed to love. The subsequent explosion of hate and the drive for revenge take the form of murder and mutilation. By the end of the movie the hate-driven Roy attains full ascendancy over the now-repressed good boy Aaron. Roy tells us, "There is no Aaron," heaping on his lost good and loving self the contempt once received from the father. The masochist becomes the sadist.

In clinical experience we also come across situations where a later trauma, often humiliation at the hands of authority figures, results in the splitting off and defensive repression of the good albeit victim self, with the previously hidden, vengeance-seeking self emerging ascendant. Rage at the hurtful father and contempt for the weak mother may become manifest in the condensed form of sexual acts or fantasies that entail both hurting and degrading the partner. Generally at least the tip of that iceberg had been visible from time to time before the reversal of the dominant and hidden self-states, although these behaviors have been either denied or rationalized away by those close to the patient. The characterological proximity to the narcissistic personality disorder with some paranoid tendencies is revealed in this malignant regression.

Returning to the masochistic personality disorder, we find that narcissistic issues of shame and pride are prominent. Shame is the outcome of the self-defeating behaviors, felt victimization, and consequent public failures and of the reservoir of shame fed by a primary caretaker. Therapists are acquainted with patients who have been characterized as *help-rejecting complainers*. Complaining usually has behind it a wish that someone else will remedy the cause of the complaint. The complainer is passive and victimized, yet does nothing to help herself. To do so would entail summoning up repressed aggression or "selfishness" or whatever other self-determining behavior was deemed bad either in her own fantasy or in actual parental messages in her own developmental history.

The complainer is the good one, the morally superior one. Patients whose therapy sessions are essentially complaining sessions have to be confronted with the dynamics of their playing out this way of being in the world. The therapist may collude with the char-acter defense by taking on and acting as proxy for the patient's dis-avowed aggression, forgetting the importance of neutrality. This will generally lead to protest from the patient, who cannot and will not follow the ill-conceived advice to "stand up for yourself." The intrapsychic conflict between love and hate has now become exter-nalized and transformed into a conflict between the patient and the therapist who has acted out her dark side for her. The therapist may also come from a place of acting out her own righteous anger, her own morally justified aggression in the role of proxy for the patient.

The Classical Formulation:
Moral Masochism Revisited

In her classic article "On Teasing and Being Teased: And the Prob-lem of 'Moral Masochism,'" Brenman (1952) notes the occasional difficulty of bringing clinical data together with a coherent theory of psychological organization. This is particularly true when the behavior under discussion is *"a complex configuration resulting from the interplay of: (1) primitive unconscious drives with (2) defensive pro-cesses and (3) adaptive implementations"* (p. 264). Although Bren-man's work is anchored in the theoretical orientation of her time, that is, instinct theory, her discussion involves a complicated rela-tionship setup and can be viewed with that orientation in mind. I see the conflicts of the core relationship problem as difficult to get to in the treatment of the *good girl.* Brenman writes that she "will try to demonstrate the continuity and quasi stability of personality organization which seems to be maintained in spite of monumen-tal shifts of psychic energy; and to set forth the general proposition that this continuity represents the unique configuration of the indi-vidual personality which is a persisting point of anchorage amidst the actually constant shifts of the balance of psychic forces, such shifts issuing in smaller 'subconfigurations,' some with the relative durability of character traits, others with the transient quality of passing moods" (p. 265). She views her example of teasing as one such subconfiguration. That is, the psychology of the person teased is a special case of the broader problem of *moral masochism*. What Brenman refers to as a "persisting point of anchorage," I view as the core relationship conflict.

Brenman disagrees with existing formulations concerning masochism, saying it is more than a form of instinctual expression and more than a defense mechanism. Instead she describes the observable phenomena usually subsumed under the heading of masochistic as a "highly complex set of configurations which issue from special varieties of infantile need and rage being pitted against a variety of mediating defense mechanisms and in interplay with the available *creative* or adaptive ego functions, whether these be humor, aesthetic talent or whatever" (pp. 272–273).

An Object Relationship View

The starting point of infantile need brings us directly to the relationship setup within which this need was manifest and within which it became problematic. Brenman, in keeping with instinct theory, says that the complex and infinitely toned varieties of masochistic formations express "simultaneously the unusually strong need and the consequent aggression when this need is frustrated in fact or fantasy" (p. 273). And with respect to the defense mechanisms, she observes a triad of denial, reaction formation, and introjection. She emphasizes that the use of projective mechanisms is of singular importance for masochistic formation and that the masochistic individual is ready to feel exploited by virtue of his projection of his own exploitativeness. He also projects his own hate-filled envy and becomes fearful of the envy of the other toward him. The more he sabotages his own goals so that the other will not envy him, the more he envies the other.

I would add, from an object relations perspective, that there is also projective identification in which the individual experiences the other, and in particular the therapist, as the internalized hostile and exploiting object and then attempts to control the other by a variety of behaviors. Sometimes this attempt takes the form of ingratiation. This is quite different from the false-self caretaking of the other that comes to be experienced as an identity, albeit an adaptive structure. The attempts of the masochistic personality to control are often conscious behaviors with a specific aim. This way of being in the therapeutic relationship constitutes a formidable transference resistance and has to be addressed as early as it is recognized—obviously with appropriate timing and tact. If it is not, the therapy itself becomes a kind of parody of a relationship and will be emotionally empty for both parties.

Brenman describes the power of the projective identification in the evocation of the bad internalized object by recalling the case of her patient who "maintained an unyieldingly wide-eyed expression of 'please-don't-hit-me' and would regularly spring to her feet like a jack-in-the-box in a caricature of deference if the examiner had occasion to rise during the interview. Gradually, her own therapist and to some degree other staff members began to tease her. . . . It was as if everyone felt in her unprovoked look of terror and pleading, an unjustified accusation of evil intent and an undefined implicit demand" (p. 266).

Today we speak of such events in the treatment situation as enactments in which the early self and object relationship conflict is replayed with the unconscious collusion of the therapist.

The Insistence on Goodness and the Mythical It

Brenman speaks to the paranoid element when she speaks of a "benevolent paranoid attitude, where the usual *denials* of, and *reaction formation* against, hostile impulses are projected wholesale and people are seen as essentially good and without malice, the Pollyanna-ism so familiar in the masochist" (p. 273).

I find that the individual holds on to the belief that the other is good and will be good to the self "if I just do it right." The individual denies the separateness of the psyche of the other because to acknowledge this would be to lose the illusion of being able to control the goodness and the badness of the other. I point out in the therapeutic work that there is no "it," no magical act that will fix everything, no way of being that will have magical power over the object. Belief in the mythical "it" must itself be addressed as part of an individual's magical, omnipotent fantasies.

Gender Differences

Although this observation is admittedly clinically anecdotal, over the years in my own work and in that of therapists I have supervised or who have consulted with me, the preponderance of moral masochism has been noted in women. Conversely, the preponderance of perverse, sadomasochistic sexual fantasies has been observed in men. In his clinical research, Stoller (1975) found this gender difference arising from problems within the mother-infant symbiosis and subsequent problems with gender identity.

Freud's view of masochism "as an expression of the feminine nature, and as a norm of behavior" ([1924] 1961a, p. 161) has rightfully been rejected. Moreover, noting that moral masochism occurs more often in women does not carry the same implications as Freud's view and should not be construed as doing so. All kings are men, but not all men are kings. Consider the parallel situation that although uncertainty about gender identity is observed to be more prevalent in males than in females, such uncertainty is not the norm of masculine nature. The issue here is *pathological* outcomes in development and why expression of the core relationship conflict takes the several paths that it does.

The Good Girl and the Good Boy

There seem to be more good girls than good boys. This is not to say that good boys have not been found. In the cases I have noted, the patient stays overly close to his mother, adapting to her needs and expectations. When he does rebel, it tends to be in secret, where he does an end run around his conscience. This way of being with his mother will most likely be acted out in the transference until and unless it is confronted. To get hold of this particular transference resistance and what it means will require attention and perseverance from the therapist.

Often the adaptation to maternal demands and expectations will later be experienced as superego demands, and the therapist will be reminded of the classical formulation of id-superego conflict. An unrelenting ego ideal that follows the dictum that life must be dedicated to the good and welfare of others leaves no room for the individual's own pleasure or desires. Even going scuba diving is justified by virtue of its contribution to good health. It is a right thing to do. Nagging feelings of being taken advantage of, of being a sucker, so to speak, are discounted and pushed away. Although wondering why he lets himself be so abused, the individual acknowledges that this way of being in the world does leave him feeling morally superior. Although the classical analytic formulation emphasizes the role of the father in superego formation, the tenacity of this overly moral stance speaks to its function of keeping him connected with the mother.

The core relationship problem for this individual is the unreliability or loss of the mother's genuine emotional bond with what Winnicott ([1960] 1965a) would call his true self. In the case of the masochistic personality disorder this breach takes place in the third year, with less devastating effects on personality development than those abandonments that take place in the first two years. Later in life the individual backs away from a committed relationship with a woman, anticipating that he will become hostage to her demands and expectations. We may see the alternation of his masochistic submission with his secret rebellion or actual withdrawal from the relationship. For both the good girl and the good boy the emotional unavailability of the father leaves the child feeling trapped within the mother's orbit, which intensifies the child's conflict vis-à-vis the mother. Any attempt to move toward the father presents the child with frustrated yearning.

The Pseudo-Schizoid Defense:
The Boy's Flight from Relatedness

We have to keep in mind the developmental task faced by the little boy as he pulls himself away from his primary bond and identification with his mother, not only in the service of autonomy but
also in the service of establishing his male gender identity. Elsewhere (1989a) I have described the *pseudo-schizoid* defense of the
little boy, which supports his striving toward autonomy and toward
maleness. We can postulate that if the father is experienced as hurt-
fully rejecting or dangerous and the boy does not have a safe alternative to the mother at the time of his denial of the affectional
bond to the mother, fantasies laden with gender-sexual issues may
sometimes take the place of the now-denied attachment and yearning. This is more likely to occur when both attachments are highly
conflicted. Greenson ([1968] 1978) wrote of the importance for the
boy of disidentifying from his mother and counteridentifying with
his father in the process of establishing male gender identity.
Greenson asks if it is not in this area that we can find an answer to
why so many men are uncertain about their maleness, also point-
ing out that fetishism is almost 100 percent a male disease.

Coates (1989), who studied boys with gender-identity disorders, notes the importance of biological-morphological factors as
critical organizers in male gender-identity formation. She also
demonstrates the power of interpersonal factors, if not to override
the biological organizers, then at least to seriously interfere with
them. The centrality of the penis in the boy's sense of maleness, as
a morphological organizer of his sense of self, is usually evident in
male fantasies. For some men, watching pornographic videos while
masturbating takes the place of attachment and love and at the
same time confirms their sense of maleness. We need to identify
and articulate the relationship, gender-identity, and sexuality-laden
compromise formation that is embedded in these fantasies. That is,
we have to tease apart these separate developmental threads and
the conflict, anxiety, and defense associated with each of them.

This is essential if we are to make the complex personality feature amenable to analysis. Associated fantasies are frequently sado-masochistic in theme, with the patient in the masochistic position, although paradoxically he feels powerful by virtue of his ability to control the fantasy itself. He will not be hurt any more than he wants to be. In these fantasies, there is no attachment, and part-ners, real or imagined, are faceless and interchangeable. The little girl who has a firmly established gender identity creates fantasies that are essentially relational, and she plays them out through her way of being in relation to others. Although she may be conflicted about being female, her feminine identity is nevertheless estab-lished within the primary object relations matrix.

I have noted that the woman who has gender-identity confu-sion frequently was her father's quasi-son when he had none in reality. It is as if, in order to capture the oedipal father, she had to partially renounce her established femaleness. Her dreams and fantasies may reveal the wish not only for the lost mother but also for the renounced and thus lost feminine self. The sense of spe-cialness as father's favorite, albeit as a boy, can only partially com-pensate for what was given up. Her yearnings are near the surface and are relational.

Both boy and girl are derailed at the same place on the devel-opmental continuum, where the salience of the negative side of an intense ambivalence impedes healthy forward psychological move-ment. The good girl becomes stuck in a quasi-symbiotic, dependent masochistic position vis-à-vis her objects while the boy may move defensively into a pseudo-schizoid, gender-protecting cul-de-sac of sexual fantasy and obsession.

Analytic therapy will have to address the core relationship con-flict and the flight from ambivalence. Because the developmental stage of emotional derailment is later than it is for the paranoid per-sonality disorder or the narcissistic personality disorder, we do not run into the same difficulties as we have in the work with the more primitive character structure. Despite the expected defenses and resistances, there is a cohesive self and the availability of an observing ego on which to rely.

A relative of interminable therapy and the negative therapeutic reaction is the situation of the individual who is "wrecked by success." This dynamic is explored from the perspective of the core relationship problem in the following chapter.

Chapter Seventeen

"Those Wrecked by Success" Revisited

Envy and the Fear of Being Envied

As I continue to explore the many kinds of patients and the kinds of clinical problems they present to us as therapists, I follow the thread of the core relational problem. Once again this chapter shows how pursuit of that problem opens up the work, even in the most puzzling and difficult of circumstances. This is true even for the people Freud described as "those wrecked by success."

Freud ([1916] 1957b) noted how bewildering it is to find that "people occasionally fall ill precisely when a deeply-rooted and long-cherished wish has come to fulfillment. It seems then as though they were not able to tolerate their happiness" (p. 316). Freud was bound by his assumption that it is frustration that induces illness. Once we have set up a predetermined explanation for what we observe, there can be little outcome other than a skewing of our thinking toward that explanation. If we write the last page of our novel first, the entire story must lead toward that conclusion.

Freud did note that external frustration is not per se pathogenic. It is the frustration that results from internal conflict that is the problem. He wrote further that "analytic work has no difficulty in showing us that it is forces of conscience which forbid the subject to gain the long hoped-for advantage from the fortunate change in reality. It is a difficult task, however, to discover the essence and origin of these judging and punishing trends" (p. 318). And Freud's discussion of the literary characters created by Shakespeare and Ibsen led him to the conclusion that "psycho-analytic work teaches us that the forces of conscience which induce illness in consequence of success, instead of, as normally, in consequence of frustration, are closely connected with the Oedipus complex, the relation to father and mother—as perhaps, indeed, is our sense of guilt in general" (p. 331).

Though Freud understood the interpersonal origins of the Oedipus complex, once he saw things in terms of his structural paradigm, in terms of conscience—that is, superego—and guilt, he lost the relational implications of the unresolved conflict in the here and now. The closest he came to the relational outcome was in describing the fear of being castrated as punishment for oedipal desires. That fear, however, did not pertain to the relationship itself.

In my view, whether fear is the fear of someone's jealousy or envy or the fear of losing someone's love, it is a relationship problem that continues to affect the individual's way of being in the world and often stands in the way of the individual's ability either to achieve or to tolerate success. This chapter illustrates this kind of relationship problem by highlighting the clinical issue of envy and the fear of being envied.

The Dynamic of Envy

Envy rests upon a single cardinal rule: "I am *not allowed* to have what you have. It belongs to you. To have it, I must kill you or steal it from you." Envy is part of a core relationship problem. In its most derivative form, envy is projected into the universe itself, becoming the "evil eye." We knock on wood or utter the magical phrase *kine-ahora* to ward off this frightening other-symbol. Perhaps we even attribute the quality to God. The meek will inherit the earth. No one envies the meek.

Envy comes to the fore developmentally at the point at which the toddler experiences the loss of infantile illusions of omnipotence and comes to realize how dependent he is on the powerful mother and on the father as well. Their willingness to allow and promote the child's sense of identity, autonomy, adequacy, and feelings of mastery—what I call *intrinsic power* (Horner, 1989b)—

makes it unnecessary for him to develop compensatory illusions of his own power. He can safely rely on theirs to keep him safe and to help him grow. However, if they do not promote and support these feelings and self-experiences in the child and he comes to believe that only they can have any power in the relationship setup, he will envy and even hate their power.

Racker (1957) noted that prerequisite to envy is a painful recognition that one lacks what the other has. In my view the added dictum "and you have no right to it" is the sine qua non for setting up the envy dynamic.

Etchegoyen and colleagues (Etchegoyen, Lopez, and Rabih, 1987) write that envy is "an exquisitely irrational phenomenon, insofar as it pursues no other serviceable end than that of attacking what is valuable in the other, including his capacity of giving it to us" (p. 50). The patient is blocked in his wish to take the therapist as a model or even to acknowledge the usefulness of the therapist's help because to take from the therapist at all is to acknowledge what the therapist has and that increases the envy. Etchegoyen, Lopez, and Rabih point out that envy ultimately *must* spoil what is good. The person who was seen as good automatically becomes bad because of the very fact that he or she evokes envy. Thus what is good is made bad, and what is bad and thus not to be envied becomes paradoxically good.

The major difference between envy and admiration, with both denoting a looking-up attitude toward the other, is the degree of belief in the availability to the self of that which is looked up to. The more attainable the other's qualities or achievements, the more the other stands as a model to be admired. Conversely, if what is looked up to is in some way forbidden to the self, envy will result.

"Wrecked by Success"

With respect to the patient "wrecked by success" and that patient's envy and fear of being envied, the therapist considers the core relationship situation and the degree to which the parent or parents could not tolerate the expanding and successful child and, out of their own envy, either stole the child's success to make it their own, taking credit for it, or diminished the value of the child's accomplishment so as not to feel diminished in comparison or envious themselves. That is, they spoiled what they envied. Klein ([1957] 1975) would say that envy first originates in the infant's envy of the breast. In Racker's terms, a dynamic, relational understanding points to the role of the parent in defining what the child accomplishes as good or bad. This family dynamic tends to be intergenerational.

Though some individuals fall ill, wrecking what they have accomplished to ward off the anticipated and feared envious hatred, others head the entire problem off at the pass by sabotaging themselves and their efforts, to ensure there will be no success to start with. The self-sabotage wards off the envious hatred of the other. Unfortunately, the malignant dynamic does not stop there. Now the individual sees others as able to have what is forbidden to her, and her envy and envious hatred take hold. There are two kinds of projection: first the projective identification in which she relates to the other as if the other were indeed the envious parent, and second, the projection of *her own* envy. At both ends she is separated from meaningful connection with the other by the wall of negative affect that accompanies the envy, regardless of where it is perceived as originating from at the moment. Seeing others get along with one another while she is separated from them by virtue of her own dynamics stirs up jealousy of what they have with one another, anger at perceiving herself to be left out, and envy of their ability to be close. The ancient Athenian philosopher Antisthenes wrote, "As iron is eaten by rust, so are the envious consumed by envy." It is perhaps one of the most pernicious of dynamics.

There is no doubt that if a person allows herself to have the success of which she is capable, she will meet up with envy in the world. It is as certain as death and taxes. It is her response to it that makes the difference in how she lives her own life. With resolution of her own conflict involving envy and the fear of being envied, she can truly let it be the other's problem. Although she may experience loss as a consequence, tolerating that loss is a necessary aspect of the resolution of this core relationship problem. I have noted that in a number of cases, as the individual's success begins to thrive, she becomes extremely anxious at the prospect of being hated and ostracized, not only in her family but with peers as well. Helping her separate the pain of the actual circumstances from overgeneralization of the family taboo on her success in the world at large may stop her from acting out with self-sabotage in response to a reactivated core relationship problem.

In the current economics of mental health services the advent of managed care has changed the way in which many therapists have been forced to work. Far from putting aside sound clinical principles, we must apply them all the more carefully if we are to maximize our ability to help out patients in this situation. The concept of dealing with the core relationship problem is especially important in this essentially deviant frame. How to do so is the subject of the next chapter.

Chapter Eighteen

Managed Care as a Clinical Issue

Therapists today work with the Damoclean sword of managed care's yea or nay hanging over their heads. Many find themselves pleading on behalf of the patient for "more" with the trepidation of an Oliver Twist facing an unyielding and punitive Mr. Bumble. Although the patient is ostensibly kept out of the therapist-insurer loop, in truth he is ensnared in it from the start. The fate of his therapy and thus the prospect of achieving his goals for treatment can be seriously compromised without his being aware of the health care structure within which, willy-nilly, he is caught, a structure that in itself may complicate or reinforce his core relationship problem.

Countertransference difficulties may also be generated, with the therapist feeling frustrated, impotent, and rageful toward the person he has to deal with at the other end of the telephone or resentful of the patient who puts him in the middle by relying on insurance in the first place. There may be anxiety that the anticipated anger of the patient who is denied treatment will be focused on the therapist.

The patient knows his treatment is being covered by a managed care program and, under the required informed consent, must know how many sessions he is entitled to and how permission will have to be obtained by the therapist from the *gatekeeper*, if the patient is to be given additional sessions. Instead of denying this proverbial elephant in the room, the therapist has to confront its

149

presence head-on, to take it up as a issue for the treatment, as it will be relevant to a given individual's core problems.

Brief Therapy Principles and Managed Care

Brief therapy has as one of its principles the formulation of a focus during the first session and the agreement between patient and therapist to stay within that focus for a given number of meetings. It is the careful staying with the focus, with the core problem that ties together the patient's presenting issue, that makes brief therapy possible. If we and our patients stray down other interesting paths away from the focus, we may be pulled in the direction of a long-term treatment. For example, if the focus of the time-limited work is loss, the therapist at the start brings up how loss is built into the structure of the work and attends to it throughout the work.

Analogously, I suggest the integration of the existence of the managed care gatekeeper and his or her power into the work when that factor relates to the individual's core relationship conflict or problem. That is, we refer to what is laid out in the informed consent discussion and bring in what is relevant to the individual's core problem. It is a fiction to believe that the traditional dyadic setup of patient and therapist even exists under these conditions. For example, a system could be set up in which the transferentially powerful parent in the person of the therapist is revealed as weak and powerless vis-à-vis the absent parent—the managed care father who controls the family money or the mother who demands a premature self-sufficiency and who refuses to allow for rapprochement refueling. To proceed with the work as if the powerful absent parent does not exist may re-create for some patients the early family atmosphere of secrets, mystification, and denial of reality.

Using the individual patient's specific core relationship conflict or problem as an organizing principle to find the meaning of the realities of this gatekeeper-therapist-patient "family" system will also bring out the possibly hidden transference issues vis-à-vis the therapist. These transferences may be consciously or unconsciously reasoned away by the patient who, most reasonably, seems to understand and accept the realities of the treatment limits imposed by the managed care ruling. Bringing the core conflict into the treatment will probably also be helpful in dealing with the countertransference reactions, making the necessity of having to work under these conditions less frustrating and less stressful.

Therapists who are unfamiliar with the principles and techniques of brief therapy and who work with managed care referrals would do well to acquaint themselves with the brief approach. When we accept a referral that is time limited, we cannot make promises based on principles and goals of long-term treatment, promises we cannot deliver.

How the Managed Care Structure Abets Defenses

A man in his late thirties was referred by managed care with a presenting problem of failed love relationships, including two marriages. He had been seen fifteen times in a managed care situation, and the therapist was at a loss to see what could be done in five or even fifteen more sessions.

The therapist learned that after a short period of involvement, the patient would lose both sexual and emotional interest and leaves the relationship. Exploration revealed that he was bound by loyalty to his mother: "I can't let go of her and she can't let go of me." If he left her for another woman, he would experience guilt at abandoning his mother and anxiety at her retaliatory abandonment. We might surmise that a real connection with his female therapist would bring that bind to the fore and would be the basis for resistance to the transference (not letting it develop), resistance to a meaningful connection to her. In fact the therapist did complain of not feeling connected to the patient.

If the core relationship problem were articulated, perhaps the managed care gatekeeper could be identified as a quasi-proxy for the mother, reinforcing her demand that he not get attached to another woman. Furthermore, with the built-in time limit imposed by managed care, the patient is certainly not going to risk becoming attached only to be abandoned for all practical purposes. This could be brought into the work as an example in the here-and-now of a major characterological defense mechanism.

The built-in time limit also could protect the patient from experiencing the anxiety that the therapist will become as needy and possessive as his mother and not let him go. In a situation like this, where entrenched characterological defenses protect the patient from unconscious interpersonal dangers, it may not be possible to join the core relationship problem without bringing in the structure imposed by managed care.

The Deviant Frame

One often hears the statement "everything is grist for the therapy mill." It applies, among other things, to whatever idiosyncracies may be inherent in the *deviant frame*. Managed care certainly fits what one might describe as a deviant frame; one that has unsafe boundaries, absence of confidentiality, a castrated therapist who cannot be relied on, the arbitrary use of power by an unconfrontable authority figure, or the imminent danger of abandonment. In this frame it is incumbent on the therapist to identify as quickly as possible the individual's core relationship conflict and the aspect (or aspects) of the deviant frame most likely to exacerbate that individual's negative perception of the world and the people in it. This identification can be brought forward by the therapist in order to be able to work with the core relationship conflict in the here-and-now and the transference issues then interpreted.

Whatever modality we may work in, understanding that human development takes place within an interpersonal milieu and recognizing that the connection with the primary caretaker is the linchpin of the psyche will help us organize our experience of being with the individual we call our patient. Our ways of working as therapists may take us in different directions with different meta-phors and vocabularies, but the ways in which we and our patients are universally human should enable us to transcend the differences in the ways in which we are uniquely individual.

Part Four

For Supervisors Only

Chapter Nineteen

Core Relationship Problems and the Supervision Process

The supervisory relationship between a psychotherapist and his teacher or consultant is a unique one. It is not the same as patient and therapist, and although countertransference difficulties the therapist is having with his patient are part and parcel of the work, in my view it is not appropriate to turn supervision into therapy. However, identifying the nature of those difficulties is germane, separating those that should be taken to the therapist's own therapist from those that directly relate to the patient's dynamics. Especially relevant is the patient's use of projective identification in which certain reactions are evoked *in the therapist*. If properly understood by that therapist, this identification can be the source of information about what is being acted out by the patient vis-à-vis the therapist. The dynamic may be played out between supervisor and therapist in what is called parallel process.

Parallel Process

Parallel process has come to be understood as a specific kind of acting out by the supervisee in which he replicates with the supervisor what is going on with the patient in treatment. It is specific to

The author gratefully acknowledges permission to base this chapter on an earlier version that appeared in the *Clinical Supervisor*, 1988, 6, 3–12, under the title "Developmental Aspects of Psychodynamic Supervision: Parallel Process of Separation and Individuation."

the nature of the transference-countertransference in question and is usually a situation of impasse or resistance. For example, using the mechanism of projective identification, the patient might project her helpless self into the therapist who, becoming the pathological container for that helplessness, brings it to the supervisor, projecting into the supervisor the omnipotence that is the counterpart of the helplessness. Unless the supervisor is aware of what is going on, she may take on the projected omniscience or omnipotence, reinforcing the supervisee's self-experience of helplessness and inadequacy. Embedded in the acting out both in the therapy session and in the supervisory session in this runaway situation, we would find the patient's core relationship problem, how it activates the therapist's core relationship problem, and how the supervisor's core relationship problem is then also activated. Once the supervisor finally recognizes the complex interaction within this three-person matrix, it is important that she do more than name it. It is useful for the supervisor to spell out the relationship patterns that have been played out through parallel process ("Just as you inadvertently colluded with your patient by taking on the feelings of helplessness she had as a child, I colluded with you by taking on the counter-role of the parent who knows everything. Isn't it interesting how parallel process has played out here with us today?") This does not call for inappropriate self-disclosure, however.

It is always incumbent on us as therapists and therapist teachers to be aware of our own inner workings and to continue to work through old problems that may reappear from time to time. The supervisor also points out to the supervisee the importance of identifying what has been activated and of bringing it back to the supervisee's own therapist. Then the focus can go back to the patient, to identify what core relationship problem is being played out in treatment.

The supervisor, whose own need to always know may be based on developmental anxieties involving the early caretaker, can readily be caught up either in defensive omniscience or in a panic-ridden state of not knowing. Either instance makes the

supervisor a ready receptacle for projections and a likely partici-
pant in enactments.

Therapist's Developmental Tasks and Supervisor's Role

The tasks of supervisees and students are not unlike those of the
adolescent: that is, not only are they motivated to learn but in the
process they are also striving toward professional individuation,
toward emancipation from the authority of teachers and supervisors, and toward a solidification of their professional identification
within their sense of self. Although there may be unresolved relationship conflicts still to be dealt with, the tasks of professional
development that confront the supervisee are, we assume, being
met by men and women with a relatively evolved psychic structure,
despite the regressive aspects of being a student or supervisee under
the authority of teachers and supervisors. The failure of teachers
and supervisors to treat these men and women with respect, the
arbitrary or sadistic use of power, and the use of students as pawns
in the power politics of the institution have no place in the mental health professions. Not only do teachers and supervisors stand
as models for interpersonal interaction but such attitudes toward
power can be as destructive to the development of the young professional as they are to a developing child. Rationalizations supporting them are unacceptable.

When unresolved core relationship problems in the therapist
are relatively circumscribed, with the availability of an observing
ego and a conflict-free sphere of intellectual functioning, adequate
treatment and supervision may enable this individual to pursue his
professional goals with a reasonable expectation of success. However, if the supervisor is needed as a selfobject to the therapist, in
order to maintain the therapist's self-cohesion and positive self-
feeling, the educational process will be seriously compromised. Furthermore, the same vulnerabilities are likely to interfere with that
therapist's ability to do the clinical work.

Conflicts

The main conflicts that may be activated in the therapist-supervisor relationship will involve dependency versus autonomy; they will involve power issues—with either one person's need to be in the position of power or one person's refusal to take healthy power and need to stay in defensive powerlessness—and they will involve the competitive dynamic of the oedipal situation.

The guilt and anxiety of the unresolved oedipal situation may lead to a renunciation of healthy power, which then leads to diminished self-esteem alongside envy and resentment of the other who is allowed to have power. Or this guilt and anxiety may lead to an exaggerated competitiveness and a need to defeat the rival at all costs in order to restore the self-esteem lost in the original oedipal defeat. Indeed, both postures can and do exist side by side in the same individual, with security and self-esteem perennially at odds with one another. With a sense of shame, the individual renounces power in order to preserve the rival who is also loved and needed, while a murderous competitiveness is displaced and played out in an effort to undo the shame.

The supervisor is in a different position from that of the therapist in this kind of situation. The supervisor is expected to have wisdom or knowledge or experience that makes it possible to help the less experienced or less knowledgeable supervisee and also to *communicate* this wisdom, knowledge, or experience. These qualities cannot be put aside in order to act as a selfobject for the supervisee, as one would do if one were the supervisee's therapist. It requires inordinate skill and tact for the supervisor to teach and at the same time to support the supervisee's sense of competence and esteem. When there are unresolved core relationship problems on *both* sides of this interpersonal equation, the supervisory experience will be unsatisfactory for both participants.

At a disadvantage vis-à-vis teachers and supervisors in terms of institutional power, defined knowledge and ability, and experienced mastery and competence, the beginning psychotherapist is plunged into a recapitulation of early developmental crises, with a loss of hard-won gains of adolescence and adulthood, and both security and self-esteem are rendered vulnerable to the power of the men and women who hold in their hands the professional identity and economic future of the student. His fate depends in part on the attitudes of supervisors toward power. Is it something to be used benevolently and reliably in the interest of the student's growth toward competence and autonomy, or is it to be used in the service of the supervisor's need to control, to maintain a posture of superiority, or to destroy the power of the other?

On the one hand what happens when the supervisee meets the developmental crises from a posture of passivity and helplessness? If the supervisor colludes with this defense by taking over the process in a manner that freezes supervisor and supervisee in a one-up, one-down relationship, the supervisee's healthy strivings for mastery, autonomy, and self-esteem will be blocked.

On the other hand the student may challenge the supervisor, with the prime motivation being to defeat and humiliate the powerful authority figure. The supervisor may be rendered impotent when this motive is acted out, and the situation will have to be addressed directly if the training process is to have a good outcome. It is to be hoped that the acting out of unresolved core relationship problems by the supervisee will not simply activate those of the supervisor.

Confrontation of the Core Problem

Interpretation of the supervisee's transferences to the supervisor is a treatment mode and outside the structure of the supervisory situation. The supervisor can try simply to handle the transferences with tact and skill in hopes of restoring the student's observing ego and the supervisory alliance. It is the supervisor's having a handle on her own core relationship problems so that she does not act them out that makes this a possible route to take.

Sometimes it may be necessary to confront a problem in a forthright manner to bring it into the open. The supervisor might say something like, "I have a sense that your concern with what I might say is getting in the way of your being able to really listen to your patient. Do you think this could be so?" The supervisor need not go into the deeper issues underlying the wish to please. That investigation, of course, belongs in the therapist's own therapy. However, this kind of supervisory intervention may in fact enhance the supervisee's treatment. Not only might the exploration of the impediment at this level free the supervisee to function more creatively as a therapist but the supervisor's readiness to look at interpersonal issues in the supervisory relationship serves as a model for dealing with similar issues in the treatment relationship. The concept of interpersonal process is demonstrated firsthand.

The Mentor

The mentor stands halfway between supervisor and colleague. Too often the relationship between mentor and protégé develops into a quasi-love relationship in which a mutual idealization obscures underlying issues of dominance and masochistic submission. In many such cases the setup is never resolved, and the hierarchical distinction, idealized as it may be, remains the same over years. The maturation of the junior member of the team stops in its tracks.

It is regrettably not all that rare to find this situation sexualized with a collusive acting out, a metaphor of incest with an idealized parent figure in an illusion of specialness vis-à-vis the powerful parent. But when unresolved oedipal issues lead to a persistent wish to be specially chosen and loved over the rival and to a stance of trying to please the supervisor in a variety of ways, what happens to professional goals and aspirations?

Professional Identification

Early identification with the primary attachment object is central to the structuring of the ego and contributes to psychological and emotional autonomy. The identifications with the mother and father of the postdifferentiation phases of development lead to the structuring of the superego in its functions both as conscience and as ego ideal. If the models are benevolent, the identifications will lead to the formation of a benevolent superego.

To some degree, identification with aspects of the therapist is an inevitable and perhaps intrinsic outcome of therapy in which executive modalities of the therapist are internalized by the patient in a manner that enables that patient to become his or her own therapist. This is in addition to those internalizations of the therapist as a new object in relation with a more evolved self. Along with substantive educational results in matters both theoretical and clinical, identification with aspects of the supervisor is likely to be one of the outcomes of the supervisory experience. Supervision is as much a do-as-I-do situation as it is a do-as-I-say one. The supervisee's patients will to some degree inherit the outcome of these identifications.

Identifying with the supervisor's benevolent power, the new therapist can move toward professional individuation, with emancipation from the authority of the supervisor and a solidification of identity. The supervisor's realistic attitude of respect for the woman or man who is attempting to master major emotional and intellectual challenges and the supervisor's dedication to the growth of the supervisee, makes the supervisor a reassuring support and validator of the student's strengths and achievements. This supervisor will welcome the supervisee's gradual move toward the status of colleague and friend.

References

Adelson, J. Review of Sowell's *Late-Talking Children*. *Wall Street Journal*, Aug. 25, 1997, sec. A.

Adler, M. *How to Think About God*. New York: Bantam, 1980.

Alexander, F. "Educative Influence of Personalty Factors in the Environment." In C. Kluckhohn, H. A., Murray, and D. M. Schneider (eds.), *Personality in Nature, Society, and Culture*. New York: Knopf, 1953.

Allison, G. "Motherhood, Motherliness, and Psychogenic Infertility." *Psychoanalytic Quarterly*, 1997, 66, 1–7.

Bateson, G., Jackson, D. D., Haley, J., and Weakland, J. H. "Toward a Theory of Schizophrenia." *Behavioral Science*, 1956, 1, 251–264.

Bjerre, A. *The Psychology of Murder*. New York: Da Capo Press, 1981. (Originally published 1927.)

Boszormenyi-Nagy, I., and Spark, G. *Invisible Loyalties*. New York: HarperCollins, 1973.

Bowlby, J. *Forty-Four Juvenile Thieves: Their Character and Home Life*. London: Baillere-Tindall, 1946.

Bowlby, J. "Grief and Mourning in Infancy and Childhood." *The Psychoanalytic Study of the Child*, 1960, 15, 9–52.

Bowlby, J. *Attachment and Loss*. Vol. 1. New York: Basic Books, 1969.

Brenman, M. "On Teasing and Being Teased: And the Problem of 'Moral Masochism.'" *The Psychoanalytic Study of the Child*, 1952, 7, 264–285.

Bromberg, P. "Empathy, Anxiety, and Reality." *Contemporary Psychoanalysis*, 1980, 16, 223–236.

Bromberg, P. "'Speak! That I May See You': Some Reflections on Dissociation, Reality, and Psychoanalytic Listening." *Psychoanalytic Dialogues*, 1994, 4, 517–547.

Bromberg, P. "Hysteria, Dissociation, and Cure: Treating Patients with Symptoms and Symptoms with Patience." *Psychoanalytic Dialogues*, 1996a, 6, 55–71.

Bromberg, P. "Standing in the Spaces: The Multiplicity of Self and the Psycho-analytic Relationship." *Contemporary Psychoanalysis*, 1996b, *32*, 509–535.

Calogeras, R., and Alston, T. "Family Pathology and the Infantile Neurosis." *International Journal of Psycho-Analysis*, 1985, 66, 359–373.

Coates, S. "Conflict in Gender in Boys." Paper presented at the meeting of the American Academy of Psychoanalysis, New York, Jan. 1989.

Cummings, E. E. *E. E. Cummings: Complete Poems: 1904–1962.* (Rev. ed.) (G. J. Firmage, ed.) New York: Liveright, 1991.

Eissler, K. "On Some Theoretical and Technical Problems Regarding the Payment of Fees for Psychoanalytic Treatment." *International Review of Psycho-analysis*, 1974, *1*, 73–102.

Erikson, E. "Observations on the Yurok: Childhood and World Image." *American Archeology and Ethnology*, 1943, *35*(4).

Erikson, E. *Childhood and Society.* New York: Norton, 1950.

Etchegoyen, R., Lopez, B., and Rabih, M. "On Envy and How to Interpret It." *International Journal of Psycho-Analysis*, 1987, 68, 49–61.

Fantz, R. "Pattern Discrimination and Selective Attention as Determinants of Perceptual Development from Birth." In A. J. Kidd and J. L. Rivoire (eds.), *Perceptual Development in Children.* Madison, Conn.: International Universities Press, 1966.

Fogel, A. "Affect Dynamics in Early Infancy: Affective Tolerance." In T. Field and A. Fogel (eds.), *Emotions and Early Interaction.* Hillsdale, N.J.: Erlbaum, 1982.

Framo, J. "Symptoms from a Family Transactional Viewpoint." *International Psychiatry Clinics*, 1970, *7*, 125–171.

Freud, S. "Extracts from the Fliess Papers." In J. Strachey (ed.), *The Standard Edition*, Vol. 1: *Pre-Psycho-Analytic Publications* and *Unpublished Drafts*. London: Hogarth, 1953a. (Originally published 1894.)

Freud, S. *The Standard Edition.* Vol. 4: *Interpretation of Dreams.* (J. Strachey, ed.) London: Hogarth, 1953b. (Originally published 1900.)

Freud, S. "Totem and Taboo." In J. Strachey (ed.), *The Standard Edition*, Vol. 13: *Totem and Taboo* and *Other Works*. London: Hogarth, 1953c. (Originally published 1913.)

Freud, S. "The Future Prospects of Psycho-Analytic Therapy." In J. Strachey (ed.), *The Standard Edition*, Vol. 11: *Five Lectures on Psycho-Analysis, Leonardo da Vinci*, and *Other Works*. London: Hogarth, 1957a. (Originally published 1910.)

Freud, S. "Some Character-Types Met With in Psycho-Analytic Work: Those Wrecked by Success." In J. Strachey (ed.), *The Standard Edition*, Vol. 14: *On the History of the Psycho-Analytic Movement, Papers on Metapsychology*, and *Other Works*. London: Hogarth, 1957b. (Originally published 1916.)

Freud, S. "The Unconscious." In J. Strachey (ed.), *The Standard Edition*, Vol. 14: *On the History of the Psycho-Analytic Movement, Papers on Metapsychology, and Other Works*. London: Hogarth, 1957c. (Originally published 1915.)

Freud, S. "On Beginning the Treatment (Further Recommendations on the Technique of Psycho-Analysis I)." In J. Strachey (ed.), *The Standard Edition*, Vol. 12: *The Case of Schreber, Papers on Technique*, and *Other Works*. London: Hogarth, 1958. (Originally published 1913.)

Freud, S. "The Economic Problem of Masochism." In J. Strachey (ed.), *The Standard Edition*, Vol. 19: *The Ego and the Id* and *Other Works*. London: Hogarth, 1961a. (Originally published 1924.)

Freud, S. "The Ego and the Id." In J. Strachey (ed.), *The Standard Edition*, Vol. 19: *The Ego and the Id* and *Other Works*. London: Hogarth, 1961b. (Originally published 1923.)

Freud, S. "The Future of an Illusion." In J. Strachey (ed.), *The Standard Edition*, Vol. 21: *The Future of an Illusion, Civilization and Its Discontents*, and *Other Works*. London: Hogarth, 1961c. (Originally published 1927.)

Freud, S. "Analysis Terminable and Interminable." In J. Strachey (ed.), *The Standard Edition*, Vol. 23: *Moses and Monotheism, An Outline of Psycho-Analysis*, and *Other Works*. London: Hogarth, 1964. (Originally published 1937.)

Friedman, L. "Ferrum, Ignis, and Medicine: Return to the Crucible." *Journal of the American Psychoanalytic Association*, 1997, *45*, 21–36.

Friedman, M. "Reflections on the Buber-Rogers Dialogue." *Journal of Humanistic Psychology*, 1994, *34*, 46–65.

Gedo, J. Review of R. D. Stolorow and G. E. Atwood, *Contexts of Being: The Intersubjective Foundations of Psychological Life*. *Journal of the American Psychoanalytic Association*, 1996, *44*, 1243–1246.

Giovacchini, P. "Technical Difficulties in Treating Some Characterological Disorders: Countertransference Problems." *International Journal of Psychoanalytic Psychotherapy*, 1972, *1*, 112–128.

Greenacre, P. "Further Considerations Regarding Fetishism." *Psychoanalytic Study of the Child*, 1955, *10*, 187–194.

Greenberg, J. "Theoretical Models and the Analyst's Neutrality." *Contemporary Psychoanalysis*, 1986, *22*, 87–106.

Greenson, R. "Disidentifying from Mother: Its Special Importance for Boys." In R. Greenson, *Explorations in Psychoanalysis*. Madison, Conn.: International Universities Press, 1978. (Originally published 1968.)

Grotstein, J. "Nothingness, Meaninglessness, Chaos and the 'Black Hole.'" *Contemporary Psychoanalysis*, 1990, *26*, 257–290.

Guntrip, H. *Psychoanalytic Theory, Therapy, and the Self*. New York: Basic Books, 1971.

Hoffman, E. *The Way of Splendor: Jewish Mysticism and Modern Psychology*. Northvale, N.J.: Aronson, 1989.

Horner A. "An Investigation of the Relationship of Value Orientation to the Adaptive-Defensive System of the Personality." Unpublished doctoral dissertation. Ann Arbor, University Microfilms, 1965.

Horner A. *Object Relations and the Developing Ego in Therapy*. Northvale, N.J.: Aronson, 1984. (Originally published 1979.)

Horner A. "The Unconscious and the Archaeology of Human Relationships." In R. Stern (ed.), *Theories of the Unconscious and Theories of the Self*. Hillsdale, N.J.: Analytic Press, 1987.

Horner, A. "Developmental Aspects of Psychodynamic Supervision: Parallel Process of Separation and Individuation." *Clinical Supervisor*, 1988, 6, 3–12.

Horner A. "Pseudo-Schizoid Development: The Little Boy's Dilemma." *Journal of the American Academy of Psychoanalysis*, 1989a, 17, 491–493.

Horner A. *The Wish for Power and the Fear of Having It*. Northvale, N.J.: Aronson, 1989b.

Horner A. "Preoedipal Factors in Selection for Brief Psychotherapy." In A. Horner, *The Primacy of Structure: Psychotherapy of Underlying Character Pathology*. Northvale, N.J.: Aronson, 1990.

Horner, A. "Money Issues and Analytic Neutrality." In S. Klebanow and E. L. Lowenkopf (eds.), *Money and Mind*. New York: Plenum, 1991a.

Horner, A. *Psychoanalytic Object Relations Therapy*. Northvale, N.J.: Aronson, 1991b.

Horner A. "The Place of the Signifier in Psychoanalytic Object Relations Theory." *Journal of the American Academy of Psychoanalysis*, 1995, 23, 71–78.

Horner A. "Belief Systems and the Analytic Work." *American Journal of Psychoanalysis*, 1997, 57, 75–78.

Horney, K. *Our Inner Conflicts: A Constructive Theory of Neurosis*. New York: Norton, 1945.

Images of Mental Illness: Science Looks Inside the Brain. A forum sponsored by the California Institute of Technology and the *Pasadena Star-News* in cooperation with the Mental Health Association in Los Angeles County. California Institute of Technology, Pasadena, June 1996.

Ingram, D. "Poststructuralist Interpretation of the Psychoanalytic Relationship." Paper presented at the meeting of the American Academy of Psychoanalysis, San Francisco, May 1993.

Ingram, D. "The Vigor of Metaphor in Clinical Practice." *American Journal of Psychoanalysis*, 1996, 56, 17–34.

Jacobson, E. *The Self and the Object World*. Madison, Conn.: International Universities Press, 1964.

Khan, M.M.R. "The Concept of Cumulative Trauma." *Psychoanalytic Study of the Child*, 1963, 18, 286–306.

Klein, M. "Envy and Gratitude." In M. Klein, *Envy and Gratitude and Other Works*. New York: Delacorte Press, 1975. (Originally published 1957.)

Kohut, H. *The Analysis of the Self*. Madison, Conn.: International Universities Press, 1971.

Kohut, H. *Restoration of the Self*. Madison, Conn.: International Universities Press, 1977.

Kristeva, J. *Powers of Horror: An Essay on Abjection*. New York: Columbia University Press, 1982.

Krystal, H. "Trauma and Affect." *Psychoanalytic Study of the Child*, 1978, *33*, 81–116.

Kubie, L. *Practical and Theoretical Aspects of Psychoanalysis*. Madison, Conn.: International Universities Press, 1950.

Lachmann, F. "How Many Selves Make a Person?" *Contemporary Psychoanalysis*, 1996, *32*, 595–614.

Lachmann, F., and Beebe, B. "The Contribution of Self- and Mutual Regulation to Therapeutic Action: A Case Illustration." In A. Goldberg (ed.), *Basic Ideas Reconsidered: Progress in Self Psychology*. Vol. 12. Hillsdale, N.J.: Analytic Press, 1996a.

Lachmann, F., and Beebe, B. "Three Principles of Salience in the Organization of the Patient-Analyst Interaction." *Psychoanalytic Psychology*, 1996b, *13*, 1–22.

Langs, R. *The Bipersonal Field*. Northvale, N.J.: Aronson, 1976.

Leavy, S. A. "Self and Sign in Free Association." *Psychoanalytic Quarterly*, 1993, *62*, 400–421.

Loewald, H. "The Waning of the Oedipus Complex." *Journal of the American Psychoanalytic Association*, 1979, *27*, 751–775.

Lorenz, K. "Der Kumpan in der Umwelt des Vogels." In C. H. Schiller (ed.), *Instinctive Behavior*. Madison, Conn.: International Universities Press, 1957. (Originally published 1935.)

Luborsky, L., Crits-Christoph, P., Mintz, J., and Auerbach, A. *Who Will Benefit from Psychotherapy? Predicting Therapeutic Outcomes*. New York: Basic Books, 1988.

Macdonald, J. *The Murderer and His Victim*. (2nd ed.) Springfield, Ill.: Thomas, 1986.

Mahler, M. *On Human Symbiosis and the Vicissitudes of Individuation*. Madison, Conn.: International Universities Press, 1968.

Mahler, M., Pine, F., and Bergman, A. *The Psychological Birth of the Human Infant*. New York: Basic Books, 1975.

Makari, G., and Shapiro, T. "On Psychoanalytic Listening: Language and Unconscious Communication." *Journal of the American Psychoanalytic Association*, 1993, *41*, 991–1020.

McDougall, J. "The Psychosoma and the Psychoanalytic Process." *International Review of Psycho-Analysis*, 1974, *1*, 437–459.

Munn, N., Fernald, L., and Fernald, P. *Introduction to Psychology*. (3rd ed.) Boston: Houghton Mifflin, 1972.

Murphy, L., and Moriarty, A. *Vulnerability, Coping, and Growth: From Infancy to Adolescence*. New Haven, Conn.: Yale University Press, 1976.

Myerson, P. "When Does Need Become Desire and Desire Need?" *Contemporary Psychoanalysis*, 1981, *17*, 607–625.

Opler, M. K. *Culture, Psychiatry, and Human Values: The Methods and Values of a Social Psychiatry*. Springfield, Ill.: Thomas, 1956.

Person, E. Review of H. K. Wrye and J. K. Welles, *The Narration of Desire: Erotic Transferences and Countertransferences. Journal of the American Psychoanalytic Association*, 1997, *45*, 265–270.

Peskin, M. "Drive Theory Revisited." *The Psychoanalytic Quarterly*, 1997, 66, 377–402.

Pizer, S. "The Distributed Self." *Contemporary Psychoanalysis*, 1996, *32*, 499–507.

Racker, H. "Contribution to the Problem of Psychopathological Stratification." *International Journal of Psycho-Analysis*, 1957, *38*, 223–239.

Renik, O. "One Kind of Negative Therapeutic Reaction." *Journal of the American Psychoanalytic Association*, 1991, *39*, 87–105.

Rutter, M. *The Qualities of Mothering: Maternal Deprivation Reassessed*. Northvale, N.J.: Aronson, 1974.

Salzman, L. *The Obsessive Personality: Origins, Dynamics, and Therapy*. New York: Science House, 1968.

Sandler, J. "Unconscious Wishes and Human Relationships." *Contemporary Psychoanalysis*, 1981, *17*, 180–196.

Schafer, R. *The Analytic Attitude*. New York: Basic Books, 1983.

Schore, A. "The Experience-Dependent Maturation of a Regulatory System in the Orbital Prefrontal Cortex and the Origin of Developmental Psychopathology." *Development and Psychopathology*, 1996, *8*, 59–87.

Shawver, L. "Postmodernizing the Unconscious." *American Journal of Psychoanalysis*, forthcoming.

Shengold, L. "Child Abuse and Deprivation: Soul Murder." *Journal of the American Psychoanalytic Association*, 1979, *27*, 533–559.

Slipp, S. "The Symbiotic Survival Pattern: A Relational Theory of Schizophrenia." *Family Process*, 1973, *12*, 377–397.

Slipp, S. *Object Relations: A Dynamic Bridge Between Individual and Family Treatment*. Northvale, N.J.: Aronson, 1984.

Stierlin, H. *Separating Parents and Adolescents: A Perspective on Running Away, Schizophrenia, and Waywardness*. New York: Quadrangle, 1974.

Stoller, R. *Perversion: The Erotic Form of Hatred*. New York: Pantheon Books, 1975.

Strachey, J. "Editor's Note." In J. Strachey (ed.), *The Standard Edition*, Vol. 14: *On the History of the Psycho-Analytic Movement, Papers on Metapsychology, and Other Works*. London: Hogarth, 1957.

Sullivan, H. *The Interpersonal Theory of Psychiatry*. New York: Norton, 1953.

Sullivan, H. "The Interpersonal Theory of Mental Disorder." In H. S. Perry,

M. L. Gawel, and M. Gibbon (eds.), *Clinical Studies in Psychiatry*. New York: Norton, 1956.

Sutherland, J. "Fairbairn's Journey into the Interior." In J. Grotstein and D. Rinsley (eds.), *Fairbairn and the Origins of Object Relations*. New York: Guilford Press, 1994. (Originally published 1989.)

Tansey, M., and Burke, W. *Understanding Countertransference: From Projective Identification to Empathy*. Hillsdale, N.J.: Analytic Press, 1989.

Van Buren, J. "Mother-Infant Semiotics: Intuition and the Development of Human Subjectivity: Klein/Lacan: Fantasy and Meaning." *Journal of the American Academy of Psychoanalysis*, 1993, *21*, 567–580.

Winnicott, D. W. "Hate in the Countertransference." *International Journal of Psycho-Analysis*, 1949, *30*, 69–75.

Winnicott, D. W. "Ego Distortion in Terms of True and False Self." In D. W. Winnicott, *The Maturational Processes and the Facilitating Environment*. Madison, Conn.: International Universities Press, 1965a. (Originally published 1960.)

Winnicott, D. W. "Ego Integration in Child Development." In D. W. Winnicott, *The Maturational Processes and the Facilitating Environment*. Madison, Conn.: International Universities Press, 1965b. (Originally published 1962.)

Winnicott, D. W. *Playing and Reality*. London: Tavistock, 1971.

Winnicott, D. W. "Fear of Breakdown." *International Review of Psycho-Analysis*, 1974, *1*, 103–107.

Winnicott, D. W. "Transitional Objects and Transitional Phenomena." In D. W. Winnicott, *Through Paediatrics to Psycho-Analysis*. New York: Basic Books, 1975. (Originally published 1951.)

Wrye, H. K., and Welles, J. K. *The Narration of Desire: Erotic Transferences and Countertransferences*. Hillsdale, N.J.: The Analytic Press, 1994.

About the Author

Althea Horner is a scientific associate of the American Academy of Psychoanalysis and an honorary member of the Southern California Psychoanalytic Institute and Society. She received her Ph.D. degree (1965) in clinical psychology from the University of Southern California. In addition to many journal articles, she is the author of *Object Relations and the Developing Ego in Therapy* (1979, 1984); *The Primacy of Structure: Psychotherapy of Underlying Character Pathology* (1990); *Psychoanalytic Object Relations Therapy* (1991); *The Wish for Power and the Fear of Having It* (1989, 1995); and *Being and Loving* (1978, 1986, 1990). In addition she is the editor of *Treating the Neurotic Patient in Brief Psychotherapy* (1985, 1994), for which she also wrote several chapters. She serves on the editorial boards of the *American Journal of Psychoanalysis*, the *Journal of the American Academy of Psychoanalysis*, and the *Journal of Humanistic Psychology*.

About the Foreword Author

Samuel Slipp is clinical professor of psychiatry at New York University School of Medicine and training and supervising analyst at the Psychoanalytic Institute of New York Medical College. He is the author of *Curative Factors in Dynamic Psychotherapy; A Glossary of Group and Family Psychotherapy; Object Relations: A Dynamic Bridge Between Individual and Family Treatment; The Technique and Practice of Object Relations Family Therapy; The Freudian Mystique: Freud, Women, and Feminism;* and *Healing the Gender Wars: Therapy with Men and Couples.*

Index